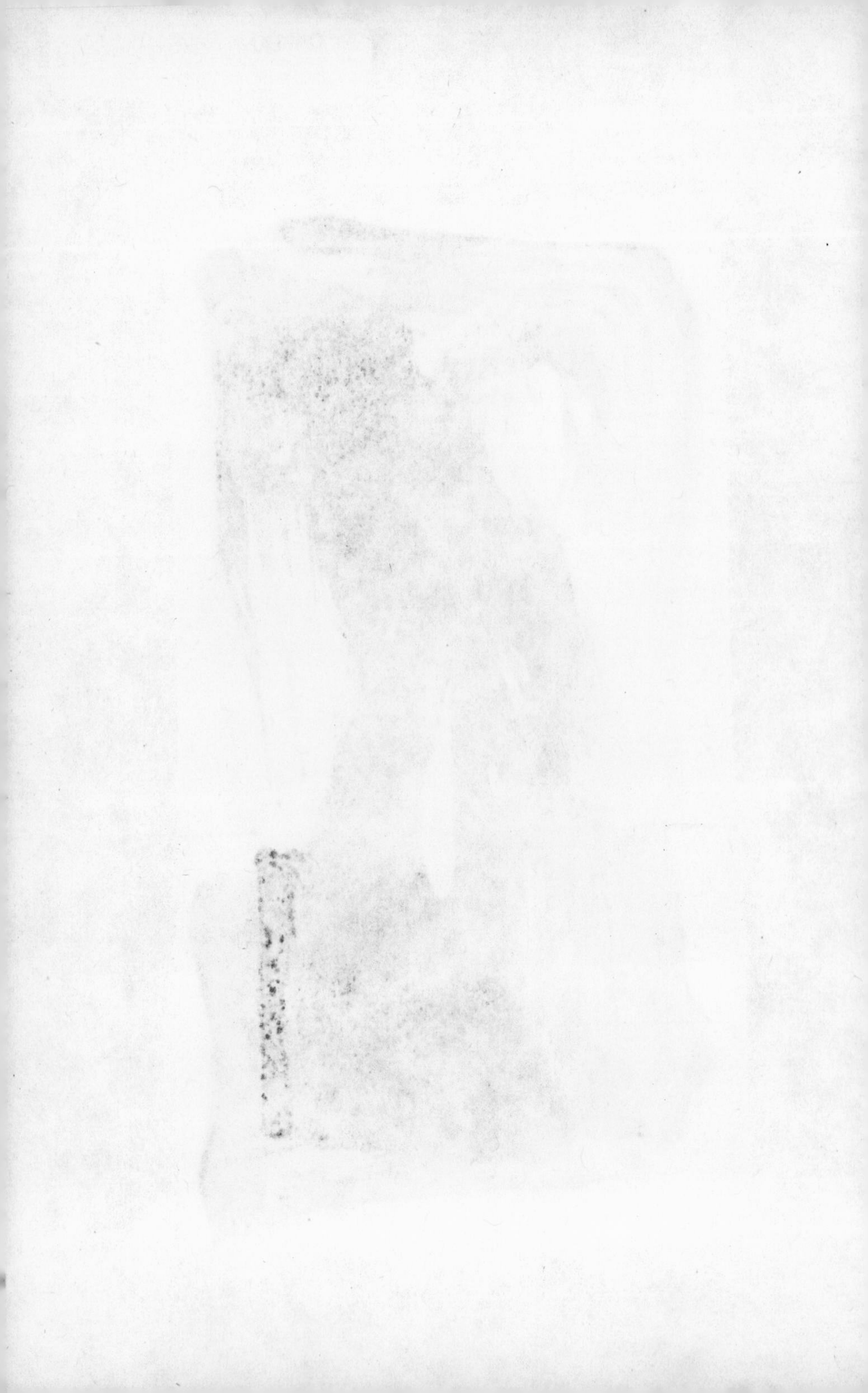

THE MINISTRY OF ART

THE MINISTRY OF ART

BY

RALPH ADAMS CRAM

LITT.D., F.A.I.A., F.R.G.S.

Essay Index Reprint Series

BOOKS FOR LIBRARIES PRESS, INC.

FREEPORT, NEW YORK

First Published 1914
Reprinted 1967

LIBRARY OF CONGRESS CATALOG NUMBER:
67-30203

PRINTED IN THE UNITED STATES OF AMERICA

To

Her Grace Adeline Marie
Duchess of Bedford

PREFACE

In bringing together for publication lectures and addresses delivered at different times, before various audiences, and in places widely separated from each other, the question inevitably arises whether they shall be printed as they were given or, instead, wholly recast through the elimination of ideas and passages that are common to several or even all of them. To follow the latter course is almost impossible without total destruction of such chain of thought as may exist, and, therefore, it seems better to rest under the charge of indulging in vain repetitions than to lay one's self open to the opposite charge of incoherency of thought.

After all, there is no longer the possibility of novelty in ideas, except where these are indefensible by any argument based on history and precedent: the fundamental laws — spiritual, ethical, philosophical — were long ago either revealed or determined, and the only excuse for their reiteration to-day is that so many of them have been forgotten and overlaid by the detritus of loose thinking, it must fall to some to rescue them from their temporary (but curiously periodic) oblivion. In bringing them forward once more, the best one can hope to do is to clothe them in some new dress that, however defective it may be, shall yet serve to arouse interest and attract attention.

So these fugitive papers must stand in their original estate, repetitions and all, on the chance that whatever things are in them worthy of attention (assuming such qualities to exist) shall at least be heard for their much speaking.

So far as the title is concerned, if any explanation or justification is necessary other than what will, I trust, appear from the contents of the essays themselves, let me say that by the words "The Ministry of Art" I mean that function which I think art has performed, and always can perform, as an agency working toward the redemption of human character; and in this aspect (which is, of course, only one of several) it takes on something of that quality which characterizes the ministers of the Christian Church.

PREFACE

From the earliest times there have always been three major orders of this ministry, bishops, priests, and deacons, who at their several ordinations receive "Character" which is indelible, which may not be repeated, and which gives them, severally, certain definite authority, with power to administer certain sacraments. These are the major orders, but there are minor orders as well, as acolytes, exorcists, readers, who, without special sacramental power, are yet definitely "ministers" of religion.

Now, as there are also seven major sacraments, which nevertheless do not in themselves take up and include all that sacramentalism which is, indeed, not only the most essential element in the Church, but also the very underlying law of life itself, extending into the farthest fringes of being, so the ministerial quality is not monopolized by the divinely established orders, but reaches out in weakening degree amongst many classes of men, whereby they themselves are, or may become, "ministers" in potency and in fact.

And this I conceive to be the highest function of the artist and the art that is his agency of operation. Not that I would for a moment make this an exclusive property; art has sufficient reason for existence in its quality as a creator of simple, sensuous joy and refreshment; as a beneficent force expressing itself through — and absolutely restricted to — pure beauty. As, however, each material thing in the universe has its sacramental quality, expressing a secret spiritual grace through an outward and visible form, from the crystalline snowflake that symbolizes the fancy of playful angels working under inexorable law, to the mind of man which is but the crude, material type of the very Mind of God, so abstract art may do more than make life beautiful (at times), in that it can act symbolically, tropically, sacramentally, and so become the supreme means of expressing, and of inciting and exalting, those emotions which transcend experience and may not in any degree find voice through those channels of expression which are entirely adequate for the purposes of the intellect.

In this aspect the master of art (the word "artist" has acquired a sickly connotation which almost rules it out of use in this connection) wields a power of most astonishing magnitude, and he may, if he likes, become through his works one of the greatest agencies of righteousness and light, and, conversely, he may too easily become the servant of damnation. That he has so often become the latter is less his own fault, perhaps, than that of society itself, which, when it periodically strikes its downward course, becomes actually poisonous, and very swiftly metamorphoses the best of arts and the most willing of artists into Circean beasts. If the master of art himself, and the world he would serve, were more clearly and persistently convinced of the great educational, expressive, and dynamic force of art as art and as a sacramental agency, it is even possible that, though they might not be avoided, the depths to which civilization periodically falls might not be so abysmal as history records, the crests more enduring and prolonged, the nodal points less closely set together.

And now again, as the descending curve meets the ascending swell and we confront a crossing of tendencies with all this ever has implied of cross-currents and confusion, it is particularly important that the higher aspects of art in all its forms should be brought to mind, while we call upon it to exercise its just and unique functions of expression and eduction. There is a new strength in all the arts, as always happens when the power that created them is losing force, and while this cannot possibly arrest the fall of one dynasty or the rise of the other, it has a great part to perform, if it wholly realizes itself, in giving expression to all that is worth preserving in an era so fast becoming history, and in bridging the inevitable chasm now opening between one definite epoch and the next. In the interregnum we may expect a general breakdown of what we now consider a triumphant civilization, but the artist has the same part to play here that was so splendidly performed by the monasteries of the Dark Ages. In his work, whatever it may be, he must record and preserve all that was and is best in a shattered era, that this may be carried over into the next and play its new part, no longer of conservation but of re-creation.

So, in a sense, the artist stands as a minister in minor orders, and so his life and acts take hold of that sacramentalism that is the foundation of both the Church and the world: if he plays his part honestly and as one so charged with duties and privileges, he may see the art to which he is sworn become once more, not only a great recorder of true civilization, but the surety of its eventual restoration.

RALPH ADAMS CRAM.

WHITEHALL,
SUDBURY, MASSACHUSETTS.

CONTENTS

THE MINISTRY OF ART

I

ART THE REVEALER

THE MINISTRY OF ART

I

ART THE REVEALER[1]

AFTER what fashion shall I, follower of art in a sense, speak on this debatable subject, here at the inauguration of a great institution of culture and learning, and before you, its earliest and forever most honoured guests, who personally and officially represent Church, State, and School, and here and now pay tribute to that great power whose duty it is to lead onward and forward every child born of man, until, man at last, he is worthy to play his part in the life that opens before him of service and charity and righteousness and worship.

I might speak of art historically, as the perfect flowering of sequent epochs of civilization, as the evanescent record of man's power of great achievement, as a glory of history in Homer and Pheidias, in Virgil and Anthemius of

[1] Address at the inauguration of Rice Institute, Houston, Texas.

Tralles, in Ambrosian chant and Gregorian plain-song, in the Arthurian legends and the Nibelungenlied, in Adam of St. Victor and Dante, in Cimabue and Giotto and their great successors, in the cathedrals and abbeys of mediævalism, in the sculptures of Pisa and Paris and Amiens, in Catholic ceremonial, in the glass of Chartres, the tapestries of Flanders, the metal-work of Spain, in the drama of Marlowe and Shakespeare, in the music of modern Germany, in the verse of the English Victorians. I might speak of art as an ornament and amenity of life, a splendid vesture covering the nakedness of society. I might speak of it in its economic aspect, or as the handmaid and exponent of religion.

Art is so great a thing, so inalienably a heritage and a natural right of man, it has all these aspects, and more; but for the moment I narrow myself to yet another consideration, — the function of art as an essential element in education.

The adjective may strike you strangely — "an essential element" — not an accessory, an extension; but I use it with intention, though to justify such use I must hasten to disavow any reference to the teaching of art as this now obtains either in art schools or under university faculties of fine arts. It is, I admit, hard to conceive such teaching as being of necessity an integral part of any scheme of general education, — however efficient it may be when viewed in the light of its own self-determined ends, — and I should expect, from no source, endorsement of any argument for the universal necessity of an art education conceived on similar lines; but I plead for a higher, or at least broader, type of such teaching, because I try to place myself amongst those who set a higher estimate on art, conceiving it to be not an applied science or a branch of industrial training, or yet an extreme refinement of culture study, but simply an indispensable means toward the achievement of that which is the end and object of education, namely, the building of character.

There were days, and I think they were very bad old days, when it was held that education should take no cognizance whatever of character, of the making of sane, sound, honourable men and women, but only of mental training and mental discipline. Then it was said with grave assurance that it was not the province of public education to deal with religion, ethics, or morals, except from a strictly historical and conscientiously non-sectarian standpoint, and that the place for the teaching of those things was the HOME — spelled with very large capitals. After a while the compulsion of events forced a readjustment of judgments, and we became conscious of the fact that a combination of influences — amongst them our very schools themselves — had resulted in the production of homes where neither religion nor ethics was taught at all, and where conscious character building was of the most superficial nature, while the concrete results were somewhat perilous to society. Struck at last by the fact that our most dangerous criminal classes were made up of those who were thoroughly well educated, we were compelled, as Walt Whitman says, "to reëxamine philosophies and religions," and some of us came to the conclusion that if the schools were to save the day — as they certainly must and certainly could — a new vision was necessary, and that what they were set to do was the bending of all their energies and powers toward character-building, toward the making, not of specialists, but of fine men and women, and good citizens.

Under the old system the significance of art and the part it could play in education were generally ignored; it was treated either as an "extra," as a special study like Egyptology or Anglo-Saxon, and so regarded as the somewhat effeminate affectation of the dilettante, or as a "vocational course," ranking so with mining engineering, dentistry, and business science. So taught, it was, indeed, no essential element in general education, but if we are right in our new view of the province thereof it may be that our old estimate of art and its function and its significance needs as drastic a revision, and that out of this may come a new method for the teaching of art.

What is it, then, this strange thing that has accompanied man's development through all history, always by his side, as faithful a servant and companion as the horse or the dog, as inseparable from him as religion itself? this baffling potentiality that has left us authentic historical records where written history is silent, and where tradition darkens its guiding light? Is it simply a collection of crafts like hunting and husbandry, building and war? Is it a pastime, the industry of the idle, the amusement of the rich? None of these, I venture to assert, but rather the visible record of all that is noblest in man, the enduring proof of the divine nature that is the breath of his nostrils.

Henri Bergson says in speaking of what he calls — inadequately, I think — intuition: "It glimmers wherever a vital instinct is at stake. On our personality, on our liberty, on the place we occupy in the whole of nature, on our origin, and perhaps also on our destiny it throws a light, feeble and vacillating, but which nevertheless pierces the darkness of the night in which the intellect leaves us." Here lies the province of art, where it has ever lain; for in all its manifestations, whether as architecture, painting, sculpture, drama, poetry, or ritual, it is the only visible and concrete expression of this mystical power in man which is greater than physical force, greater than physical mind, whether with M. Bergson we call it intuition or with Christian philosophers we call it the immortal soul.

And as the greatest of modern philosophers has curbed the intellectualism of the nineteenth century, setting metes and bounds to the province of the mind, so he indicates again the great spiritual domain into which man penetrates by his divine nature, that domain revealed to Plato and Plotinus, to Hugh of St. Victor and St. Bernard and St. Thomas Aquinas. As Browning wrote, "A man's reach must exceed his grasp, or what is a heaven for," and so, as man himself, transcending the limitations of his intellect, reaches out from the world of phenomena to that of the noumenon, as he forsakes the accidents to lay hold on the substance, he finds to his wonder and amazement the possibility of achievement, or at least of approximation, and simultaneously the overwhelming necessity for self-expression. He has entered into a consciousness that is above consciousness; words and mental concepts fail, fall short, misrepresent, for again, as M. Bergson says, "The intellect is characterized by a natural inability to comprehend life," and it is life itself he now sees face to face, not the inertia of material things, and it is here that art in all its varied forms enters in as a more mobile and adequate form of self-expression, since it is, in its highest estate, the symbolic expression of otherwise inexpressible ideas.

Through art, then, we come to the revelation of the highest that man has achieved; not in conduct, not in mentality, not in his contest with the forces of nature, but in the things that rank even higher than these — in spiritual emancipation and an apprehension of the absolute, the unconditioned. The most perfect plexus of perfected arts the world has ever known was such a cathedral as Chartres, before its choir was defiled by the noxious horrors of the eighteenth century; when its gray walls were hung with storied tapestries, its dim vaults echoed to solemn Gregorians instead of operatic futilities, and the splendid and dramatic ceremonial of mediæval Catholicism made visible the poignant religion of a Christian people. And in this amazing revelation of consummate art, music was more than "a concord of sweet sounds," painting and sculpture more than the counterfeit presentment of defective nature, architecture more than ingenious masonry. Through these, and all the other assembled arts, radiated, like the coloured fires through the jewelled windows, awe, wonder, and worship, of men who had seen some faint adumbration of the Beatific Vision, and who called aloud to their fellows, in the universal language of art, the glad tidings of great joy that, by art, man might achieve, and through art he might reveal.

Now if art is, indeed, all this, — and the proof lies clear in itself, — then its place in liberal education becomes manifest and its claims incontestable. If education is the eduction of all that is best in man, the making possible the realization of all his potentialities, the building-up of personality through the dynamic force of the assembled achievements of the human race throughout history, and all toward the end of perfecting sane and righteous and honourable character, then must you make art, so understood and so taught, as integral a part of your curriculum as natural science, or mathematics, or biology. Not in dynastic mutations, not in the red records of war, not in economic vacillations, or in mechanical achievements, lies the revelation of man in his highest and noblest estate, but in those spiritual adventures, those strivings after the unattainable, those emancipations of the human soul from the hindrance of the material form, which mark the highest points of his rise, presage his final victory, and are recorded and revealed in the art which is their voicing.

The Venus of Melos, "Antigone," Aya Sophia, Gregorian music, Latin hymnology, the "Divina Commedia," Giotto's Arena Chapel, Chartres, Westminster Abbey, "Hamlet," Goethe's "Faust," "Parsifal," "Abt Vogler" — all great art, and as great art beyond price; but greater, more significant by far as living indications of what man may be when he plays his full part in God's cosmogony.

Where is art taught in this sense and to this end? I confess I do not know. Indeed, I find in many places laboratories of art industry where, after one fashion or another, ambitious youth — and not always well advised — is shown how to spread paint on canvas; how to pat mud into some quaint resemblance to human and zoölogical forms; how to produce the voice in singing; how to manipulate the fingers in uneven contest with ingenious musical instruments; how to assemble lines and washes on Whatman paper so that an alien mason may translate them, with as little violence as possible, into terms of brick and stone — or plaster and papier mâché. And I find names, dates, sequences of artists taught from textbooks, and sources and influences taught from fertile imaginations, together with erudite schemes and plots of authorship and attribution; but where shall we find the philosophy, the rationale of art, inculcated as an elemental portion of the history of man and of his civilization?

Categories, always categories; and we confuse them to our own undoing. There have been historians who have compiled histories with no knowledge of art and with scant reference to its existence; there have been artists who have taught art with no knowledge of history and with some degree of contempt for its pretensions; yet the two are one, and neither — from an educational standpoint — is intelligible without the other. It is through Homer and Æschylus that we understand Hellas; through Aya Sophia that we understand Byzantium; through Gothic art that we know mediævalism; through St. Peter's and Guido Reni that the goal of the Renaissance is revealed to us. And so, on the other hand, what, for example, is the art of the Middle Ages if we know nothing of the burgeoning life that burst into this splendid flowering? What are the cathedral builders to us, and the myriad artists allied with them, when severed from monasticism, the Catholic revival, the crusades, feudalism, the guilds and communes, the sacramental philosophy of Hugh of St. Victor, and the scholastic philosophy of St. Thomas Aquinas? We build our little categorical box-stalls and herd history in one, art in another, religion in a third, philosophy in a fourth, and so on, until we have built a labyrinth of little cells, hermetically sealed and securely insulated, and then we wonder that our own civilization is of the same sort, and that over us hangs the threat of an ultimate bursting forth of imprisoned and antagonistic forces, with chaos and anarchy as the predicted end.

Again we approach one of those great moments of readjustment when much that has been perishes, and much that was not, comes into being. For five centuries the tendencies set in motion by the Renaissance have had full sway, and as the great epoch of mediævalism ended at last in a decadence that was inevitable, so is it with our era, called of Enlightenment, the essence of which was analysis as the essence of that was synthesis. As mediævalism was centripetal, so is modernism centrifugal, and disintegration follows on, faster and ever faster. Even now, however, the falling wave meets in its plunge and foam the rising wave that bears on its smooth and potent surge the promise and potency of a new epoch, nobler than the last, and again synthetic, creative, centripetal.

No longer is it possible for us to sever being into its component parts and look for life in each moiety; for us, and for our successors, the building-up of a new synthesis, the new vision of life as a whole, where no more are we interested in isolating religion, politics, education, industry, art, like so many curious fever germs, but where once more we realize that the potency of each lies, not in its own distinctive characteristics, but in the interplay of all.

And with this vision we return to the consciousness that all great art is a light to lighten the darkness of mere activity, that at the same time it achieves and reveals. So, as art shows forth man's transfiguration, does it also serve as a gloss on his actions, revealing that which was hid, illuminating that which was obscure.

So estimated and so inculcated, art becomes, not an accessory, but an essential, and as such it must be made an integral portion of every scheme of higher education. A college can well do without a school of architecture, or music, or painting, or drama, and the world will perhaps be none the poorer; but it cannot do without the best of every art in its material form, and in the cultural influences it brings to bear upon those committed to its charge, nor can it play its full part in their training and the development of their character unless out of the history of art it builds a philosophy of art that is not for the embellishment of the specialist but for all.

"Man is the measure of all things," said Protagoras, and with equal truth we can say: Art is the measure of man.

II

THE PHILOSOPHY OF THE GOTHIC RESTORATION

II

THE PHILOSOPHY OF THE GOTHIC RESTORATION[1]

THIS is a stimulating subject that you have set me; it may lead us far — it has led me far, as you are destined to discover; for there is this about art — and particularly architecture, anyway, — it refuses to stay in its neat little category of æsthetics, and branches out amazingly until it sends its roots deep down into the beginnings of things, its flower-tipped branches high up into the free air of prophecy. You may think it ought to be easy enough for me to give you a succinct account of the erratic growth of the new Gothic spirit in architecture, from the early nineteenth-century Pugins down to the latest neo-mediævalist practising to-day; easy enough for me to content myself with what is really a very interesting history (and task enough, too, for that matter), but if you do think this you little know the provocative na-

1 Read before the Contemporary Club of Philadelphia.

ture of the subject — or the susceptible nature of your speaker. No, it is impossible to deal with the matter in a superficial way, for it is not a case of adventuring into a new wonderland of style from sheer ennui, for the sake of a new sensation: the inception and growth and culmination of the new Gothic mode is not a whimsey of chance, a sport of erratic fancy; it was and is a manifestation in art forms of a world impulse, as fundamental as that which gave itself visible form in the Renaissance, as that which blossomed in the first Gothic of the twelfth century, as that which created Aya Sophia or the Parthenon. It meant something when it happened, it means something to us to-day, it will mean more to our children; and deliberately I am going to disappoint you — I fear — by trying to show what this is, instead of telling you, and demonstrating to you in pictures, what our forbears have done, what some of us are trying to do to-day.

I am convinced there is nothing accidental in our stylistic development, or in the universe, for that matter. There was once a very wise man who, on speaking of a miracle to a friend, and being confronted by the assertion that the event was not that but rather a coincidence, devoutly said that he thanked God he was not so superstitious as to believe in coincidences. So, chaotic and illogical as our devious wanderings after the strange gods of style may be, I am disposed to think that even here we may find evidences of design, of a Providence that overrules all things for good; "an idea," as Chesterton would say, "not without humour."

For chaos is the only word that one can justly apply to the quaint and inconsequent conceits in which we have indulged since that monumental moment in the early nineteenth century when, architecturally, all that had been since the beginning ceased, and that which had never been before, on land or sea, began. A walk up Fifth Avenue in New York, from Madison Square to the Park, with one's eyes open, is an experience of some surprises and equal illumination, and it leaves an indelible impression of that primal chaos that is certainly without form, if it is not wholly void. Here one may see in a scant two miles (scant, but how replete with experiences!) treasure-trove of all peoples and all generations: Roman temples and Parisian shops; Gothic of sorts (and out of sorts) from the "carpenter-Gothic" of 1845, through Victorian of that ilk, to the most modern and competent recasting of ancient forms and restored ideals; Venetian palaces and Louis Seize palaces, and Roman palaces, and more palaces from wherever palaces were ever built; delicate little Georgian ghosts, shrinking in their unpremeditated contact with Babylonian skyscrapers that poise their towering masses of plausible masonry on an unconvincing substructure of plate glass. And it is all contemporary, — the oldest of it dates not back two generations, — while it is all wildly and improbably different.

The experience prompts retrospection, and we turn over the dog-eared leaves of the immediate past; apparently it was the same, only less so, back to the decade between 1820 and 1830, and there we find a reasonably firm foothold. Here at last, at the beginning of the century, we discover actual unanimity, and with some relief we go back century after century, tracing variations, but discovering no precedent for the chaos we have left. From time to time, even to the first Olympiad, we suddenly find ourselves at some brief period where a fight is manifestly going on; but there were never more than two parties to the contest, and this once passed, we have another four or five centuries of peaceful and unified development. Our own Colonial merges without a shock in English Georgian; this, through Inigo Jones, in the Renaissance of the Continent. A generation of warfare lands us in Flamboyant Gothic, and so to real Gothic that stretches back through logical vicissitudes to the twelfth century. Another upheaval, and in a moment we are with the Romanesque that touches Rome itself, and behind Rome lies Greece. No chaos here; definite and lawful development; infinite variety, infinite personality, and a vitality that demands a more illimitable word than "infinite." What happened, then, in 1825; what is happening now; what is going to happen, and why?

We may try for an answer, but first we must lightly run over the well-thumbed leaves again.

We all know what our own Colonial was like;

perhaps we do not fully realize how varied it was as between one section and another, but at least we appreciate its simplicity and directness, its honesty, its native refinement and delicacy, its frequent originality. It is not the same as English Georgian; sometimes it is distinctly better; and, however humble or colloquial, it is marked always by extreme good taste. If anything it improved during the almost two centuries of Colonial growth, and when the nineteenth century opened it was still instinct with life. A half-century later where were we? Remember 1850, and all that that date connotes of structural dishonesty, barbarism, and general ugliness! Here is the debatable period, and we may narrow it, for in 1810, in 1820, good work was still being done, while in 1840, yes, in 1830, the sodden savagery diluted with shameless artifice was generally prevalent. To me this decade between 1820 and 1830 is one of the great moments in architectural history, for then the last flicker of instinctive art amongst men died away, and a new period came in. Such a thing had never happened before: it is true Rome never matched Greece in perfection of art; the Dark Ages after her fall were dark, indeed; the second Dark Ages after the death of Charlemagne were equally black, while the transition from Gothic to Renaissance was not without elements of disappointment, but at none of these transitional moments were people absolutely wrong-headed, never was the work of their hands positively shameless. Even now we put their poor products in our art museums, where they are not outfaced by the splendid monuments of the great and crescent epochs. In a word, what happened about 1825 was anomalous; it happened for the first time; and for the first time whatever man tried to do in art was not only wrong, it was absolutely and unescapably bad.

I should like to deal with this matter in detail, but we have no time. In a word, what had happened, it seems to me, was this: The Renaissance had struck a wrong note — and in several things besides architecture; for the first time man self-confidently set to work to invent and popularize a new and perfectly artificial style. I am not concerned here with the question whether it was a good style or not; the point is that it was done with malice aforethought; it was invented by a cabal of painters, goldsmiths, scenic artists, and literary men, and railroaded through a stunned society that, busied with other matters, took what was offered it, abandoned its old native ways, and later, when time for thought offered, found it was too late to go back. Outside Italy there was as little desire for the new-fangled mode as there was for the doctrinal Reformation outside Germany. In France and England good taste still reigned supreme, and though the dogmatic iconoclasts took good care that the best of the old work should be destroyed and that suspicion should be cast on what — from sheer exhaustion — they allowed to remain; though for one reason and another the new Classic style came in, the good taste of the people still remained operative, and while Italy and Germany were mired in Rococo and Baroque, they continued building lovely things that were good in spite of their artificial style, because their people had not lost their sense or their taste.

It could not last, however: certain essential

elements had been lost out of life during the Renaissance and the Reformation; the Revolution — third act in the great melodrama — was a foregone conclusion. It completed the working-out of the foreordained plot, and after it was over and the curtain had been rung down, whatever had been won, good taste had been lost, and remained only the memory of a thing that had been born with man's civilization and had accompanied it until that time.

You cannot sever art from society; you cannot make it grow in unfavourable soil, however zealously you may labour and lecture and subsidize. It follows from certain spiritual and social conditions, and without these it is a dead twig thrust in sand, and only a divine miracle can make such bloom, as blossomed the staff of St. Joseph of Arimathea at Glastonbury.

Well, Alberti and Palladio and Inigo Jones had dissolved and disappeared in the slim refinements of American Colonial. What followed? For a brief time and in one or two categories of activity the spacious and delusive imitations that Jefferson more or less popularized, the style sometimes known as "Neo-

Grec," but more accurately termed — because of its wide use for Protestant meeting-houses in country districts — the "Græco-Baptist" style. You know it? — Front porticoes of well-designed, four-foot Classical columns made of seven-eighths-inch pine stock, neatly nailed together, painted white, and echoing like a drum to the incautious kick of the heel; slab sides covered with clapboards, green blinds to the round-topped windows, and a little bit of a brick chimney sticking up at the stern where once, in happier days, stood the little cote that housed the Sanctus bell.

Then came what is well called "Carpenter-Gothic," marked by the same high indifference to structural integrity, and with even less reliance on precedent for its architectural forms; a perfectly awful farrago of libelous details, — pointed arches, clustered columns, buttresses, parapets, pinnacles, — and all of the ever-present pine lumber painted gray, and usually sanded as a final refinement of verisimilitude. And with these wonderful monuments, cheek by jowl, Italian villas, very white and much balconied; Swiss chalets, and every other imaginable thing that the immortal Batty Langly, or later the admirable Mr. Downing, could invent, with, for evidence of sterling American ingenuity, the "jig-saw-and-batten" refinement of crime. We really could not stand all this, you know, and when the Centennial in Philadelphia finally revealed us as, artistically speaking, the most savage of nations, we began to look about for means of amendment. We were not strikingly successful, as is evidenced by the so-called "Queen Anne" and "Eastlake" products of the morning after the celebration; but the Ruskinian leaven was working, and a group of men did go to work to produce something that at least had some vestiges of thought behind it. There is much of this very strange product now at large; it is generally considered very awful, indeed, — and so it is — but it was the first sincere and enthusiastic work for generations, and demands a word of recognition. Its vivid ugliness is due to the fact that in the space of seventy-five years the last faintest flicker of sense of beauty had vanished from the American citizen; its intensity of purpose bears witness to the sincerity of the men who did it, and I for one would give them praise, not blame.

We are approaching — in our review — another era in the development of our architecture. Let us gather up the many strands in preparation therefor. Here were the "wild and whirling words" of Hunt, Eidlitz, Furness; here is the grave old Gothic of Upjohn's following, Renwick, Congdon, Haight, — admirable, much of it, in little country churches; here is the Ruskinian fold, Cummings, Sturgis, Cabot, — rather Bostonian, you will note; here was the old Classical tradition that had slipped very, very far from the standards of Thornton, Bulfinch, McComb, now flaring luridly in the appalling forms of Mullet's Government buildings, and the Philadelphia City Hall. Let us pursue the subject no further: there were others, but let them be nameless; we have enough to indicate a condition of some complexity and a certain lack of conviction, or even racial unity. Then the Event occurred, and its name was H. H. Richardson. The first great genius in American architecture, he rolled like an æsthetic Juggernaut over the prostrate bodies of his peers and the public, and in ten years we did have substantial unity. We were like the village fireman who did n't care what colour they painted the old tub, so long as they painted her red: we did n't care what our architecture was so long as it was Romanesque. For another ten years we had a love-feast of cavernous arches, quarry-faced ashlar, cyclopean voussoirs and seaweed decorations; village schools, railway stations, cottages, — all, all were of the sacrosanct style of certain rather barbarous peoples in the south of France at the close of the Dark Ages.

And in another ten years Richardson was dead, and his style, which had followed the course of empire to the prairies, and the alkali lands, and the lands beyond the Sierras; and a few years ago I found some of it in Japan! It was splendid, and it was compelling, as its discoverer handled it, but it was alien, artificial, and impossible, equally with the bad things it displaced. But it *did* displace them, and Richardson will be remembered, not as the discoverer of a new style, but as the man who made architecture a living art once more.

Eighteen hundred and ninety, and we start again. Two tendencies are clear and explicit. A new and revivified Classic with McKim as its protagonist, and a new Gothic. The first splits up at once into three lines of development: pure Classic, Beaux Arts, and Colonial, each vital, brilliant, and beautiful in varying degrees. The second was, and remains, more or less one, a taking-over of the late Gothic of England and prolonging it into new fields, sometimes into new beauties. So matters run on for another ten years. At the end of that time the pure Classic has won new laurels for its clean and scholarly beauty; the Beaux Arts following has abandoned much of its banality of French bad taste and has become better than the best contemporary work in France; the neo-Colonial has developed into a living thing of exquisite charm, while the Gothic advance has been no less than that of its Classical rival — or should I say, bedfellow?

And now two new elements enter; steel-frame construction on the one hand, on the other, the secessionist. The steel frame is the *enfant terrible* of architecture, but like so many of the same genus it may grow up to be a serious-minded citizen and a good father. It is n't that now; it is a menace, not only to architecture, but to society, but it is young and it is having its fling. If we can make it realize that it is a new force, not a substitute, we shall do well. When it contents itself in its own proper sphere, and the municipality says kindly but firmly, "thus far and no farther," — the "thus far" being about one hundred and twenty-five feet above street level, as in my own wise town of Boston, — then it may be a good servant. Like all good servants it makes the worst possible master; and when it claims as its chiefest virtue that it enables us to reproduce the Baths of Caracalla, vaults and all, at half the price, or build a second Chartres Cathedral with no danger from thrusting arches, and with flying buttresses that may be content beautifully to exist, since they will have no other work to do, then it is time to call a halt. The foundation of good architecture is structural integrity, and it does not matter if a building is as beautiful as the Pennsylvania Station in New York; if its columns merely hide the working steel within, if its vast vaults are plaster on steel frame and expanded metal, then it is not architecture, it is scene-painting, and it takes its place with that other scene-painting of the late Renaissance to which we mistakenly apply the name of architecture.

The secessionist — one might sometimes call him Post-Impressionist, Cubist, even — is the latest element to be introduced, and in some ways he is the most interesting. Unlike his *confrères* in Germany, Spain, and Scandinavia, he shows himself little except in minor domestic work — for at heart we *are* a conservative race, whatever individuals may be, — but here he is stimulating. His habitat seems to be Chicago and the Pacific Coast; his governing conviction a strongly developed enmity to archæological forms of any kind. Some of the little houses of the Middle West are striking, quite novel, and inordinately clever; some of the Far Western work, particularly around Pasadena, is exquisite, — no less. Personally I don't believe it is possible wholly to sever one's self from the past and its forms of expression, and it certainly would be undesirable; on the other hand, however, the astute archæology of some of our best modern work, whether Classic or Gothic, is stupefying and leads nowhere. Out of the interplay of these two much of value may arise.

And there you are: three kinds of Classic, two kinds of Gothic, skeleton-frame, and secessionist, all are operative to-day; each with its strong following, each, one admits, consummately clever and improving every day; for there is no architectural retrogression in America; there is steady and startling advance, not only in facility for handling and developing styles, but in that far more important matter, recognition of the fact that styles matter far less than style. From a purely professional standpoint the most encouraging thing is that breadth of culture, that philosophical insight into the essence of things, that liberality of judgment that mark so many of the profession to-day. Gone are the old days of the "Battle of the Styles"; the swords are beaten into pruning-hooks, and these are being used very efficiently in clearing away the thicket of superstitions and prejudices that for so long choked the struggling flower of sound artistic development. The Goth and the Pagan can now meet safely in street or drawing-room without danger of acute disorder; even the structural engineer and the artist preserve the peace (in public); for all have found out that architecture is much bigger than its forms, that the fundamental laws are the same for all good styles, and that the things that count are structural integrity, good taste, restraint, vision, and significance. No one now would claim with the clangour of trumpets that the day of victory was about to dawn for the Beaux Arts, Gothic, or steel-frame styles, or for any other, for that matter; each is contributing something to the mysterious alembic we are brewing, and all we hope is that out of it may come the Philosopher's Stone, that, touching base metal, shall turn it into refined gold — which, by the way, is the proper function of architecture and of all the arts.

Chaos then confronts us, in that there is no single architectural following, but legion; and in that fact lies the honour of our art, for neither is society one, or even at one with itself. Architecture is nothing unless it is intimately expressive, and if utterly different things clamour for voicing, different also must be their architectural manifestation. You cannot build a Roman Catholic or Episcopal church in the Beaux Arts vernacular (it has been done, but it is extremely silly); because the Church is the eternal and fundamentally immutable thing in a world of change and novelty and experiment, and it has to express this quality through the connotation of the forms it developed through a thousand years to voice the fulness of its genius that was developing simultaneously. Neither can you use the steel frame or reënforced concrete to the same ends, though this very sordid wickedness has also been perpetrated, I have grounds for believing. On the other hand, think of using the consummate art of Chartres Cathedral for a railway terminal, or the Ste. Chapelle for a stock exchange, or Haddon Hall for an Atlantic City hotel, or the Ducal Palace in Venice for a department store, or the Erechtheion for a fire-engine house. The case has merely to be stated to be given leave to withdraw, and with it goes, for the time, the talk we once heard of an "American Style." Styles come from unity of impulse; styles come from a just and universal estimate of comparative values; styles come where there is the all-enveloping influence and the vivid stimulus of a clear and explicit and compelling religious faith; and these occur, not at the moment of wild confusion when one epoch of five centuries is yielding to another, but after the change in dynasty has been effected, and the new era has begun its ascending course. The only premeditated architecture I know, the only style that was deliberately devised and worked out according to preconceived ideas, — the style of the Renaissance, — was yet not half so artificial as it looks (and as some of us would like to think), for in a sense it was inevitable, granting the postulates of the humanists and the flimsy dogmas of the materialists of the fifteenth century. It did not develop insensibly and instinctively like Hellenic and Byzantine and Gothic and Chinese Buddhist art, — the really great arts in history, — but once the great parabola of mediæval civilization curved downward to its end, once Constantinople fell, something of the sort was not to be escaped.

Now I do not feel that we shall be content

with an art of the scope of that of the Renaissance; I do not feel that we shall be content with a new epoch of civilization on Renaissance lines. There are better ways of life, and saner, and more wholesome, and after Constantinople has fallen again (God send the day quickly), so marking the end, as the other fall in 1453, five centuries ago, marked the beginning, of the epoch now nearing the moment of its dissolution, I believe all the wonderful new forces, now working hiddenly, or revealing themselves sporadically, will assemble to a new synthesis that will have issue in a great epoch of civilization as unified as ours is disunited, as centripetal as ours is centrifugal, as spiritually efficient as ours is materially efficient, and that then will come, and come naturally and insensibly, the inevitable art that will be glorious and great, because it shows forth a national character, a national life that also is great and glorious.

Reduced to its simplest terms, our architecture is seen to have had two epochs; the first the attempted conservation of a definite style which, whatever its genesis, had become an essential part of our racial character, and its complete disappearance exactly at the time when the serious and conservative nature of the people of the United States gave place, with almost equal suddenness, to a new quality born partly of political independence, partly of new and stimulating natural conditions, partly of the back-wash from Continental revolution, and above all of the swift working-out, at last, of powers latent in the Renaissance-Reformation itself. Second, the confused activities of many men of many minds, who had cut loose from tradition become moribund, and who were in the position of the puppy sent by express, whose destination could not be determined because, as the expressman said, he "had eat his tag." Communal interests, the sense of solidarity inherited from the Middle Ages (which gives us the true pattern of the only possible socialism) persisting in strange new forms even through the Renaissance epoch itself, had yielded to a crescent individualism, and architecture, like a good art, followed close to heel.

This is really all there is to our architectural history between Jamestown and Plymouth Rock at one end, and syndicalism and the

Panama Exposition at the other, and I have used many words in saying what might have been expressed in a sentence. The old solidarity in life which expressed itself for four thousand years in a succession of quite distinct, but always sequent, styles died out at last, and the new individualism of pigeonhole society and personal followings came in. What lies before us? More pigeonholes, more personal followings, more individualism, with anarchy at the end? I do not think so, but rather exactly the reverse. Architecture, I insist, is always expressive; sometimes it reveals metaphysical and biological truth, when in itself there is no truth whatever. If we built Independence Hall in Philadelphia there was something in us of the same nature, and we glory in the fact. If we built the City Hall in Philadelphia, there was something in us like that, arresting as the thought must be. If we are doing three Classics, and two Gothics, and steel-frame, and Post-Impressionism (not to mention the others) at the present moment, then that is because our nature is the same. Now, can we again prove the truth of the saying, "Ex pede Herculem," and, using our present output as the foot, (I admit the connotation is of the centipede), create the Hercules? I mean can we, from what we are doing to-day, predict anything of the future? Not of our future style; that will be what our society makes it; but of society itself? For my own part, I think we can. To me all that we are doing in architecture indicates the accuracy of the deduction we draw from myriad other manifestations, that we are at the end of an epoch of materialism, rationalism, and intellectualism, and at the beginning of a wonderful new epoch, when once more we achieve a just estimate of comparative values; when material achievement becomes the slave again, and no longer the slave-driver; when spiritual intuition drives mere intellect back into its proper and very circumscribed sphere; and when religion, at the same time dogmatic, sacramental, and mystic, becomes, in the ancient and sounding phrase, "One, Holy, Catholic, and Apostolic," and assumes again its rightful place as the supreme element in life and thought, the golden chain on which are strung, and by which are bound together, the varied jewels of action.

Everywhere, and at the very moment when our material activity and our material triumphs seem to threaten the high stars, appear the evidences that this wonderful thing is coming to pass, and architecture adds its modicum of proof. What else does it mean, that on every hand men now demand in art better things than ever before, and get them, from an ever increasing number of men, whether they are Pagans, Goths, or Vandals? What is the meaning of the return to Gothic, not only in form, but "in spirit and in truth"? Is it that we are pleased with its forms and wearied of others? Not at all. It is simply this, that the Renaissance-Reformation-Revolution having run its course, and its epoch having reached its appointed term, we go back, deliberately, or instinctively, — back, as life goes back, as history goes back, to restore something of the antecedent epoch, to win again something we had lost, to return to the fork in the roads, to gain again the old lamps we credulously bartered for new. Men laugh (or did; I think they have given it over of late) at what they call the reactionary nature and the affectation of the Gothic restoration of the moment, and they would be right if it meant what they think it means. Its significance is higher than their estimate, higher than the conscious impulses of those who are furthering the work, for back of it all lies the fact that what we need to-day in our society, in the State, in the Church, is precisely what we abandoned when, as one man, we arose to the cry of the leaders and abettors of the Renaissance. We lost much, but we gained much; now the time has come for us to conserve all that we gained of good, slough off the rest, and then gather up once more the priceless heritage of mediævalism, so long disregarded.

And that is what the Gothic restoration means, a returning to other days — not for the retrieving of pleasant but forgotten forms, but for the recovery of those impulses in life which made these forms inevitable. Do you think the Pugins in England in the early part of the nineteenth century chose to build Gothic churches because they liked the forms better than those of the current Classic then in its last estate? Not at all, or at all events, not primarily; but rather because they passionately loved the old Catholic religion that voiced itself in these same churches they took as their models. And the same is true of those of us who build Gothic churches to-day: instinctively we revolt from the strange religion that, under Medici and Borgia, built the Rococo abominations of Italy, and equally from that other religion that found adequate self-expression in the barren meeting-houses of Puritan England and America; and when again we try to restore to our colleges, as at Princeton and the University of Pennsylvania and Chicago and Bryn Mawr, something of the wonderful dynamic architecture of Oxford and Cambridge and Eton and Winchester, we do it far less because we like the style better than that — or rather those — of Columbia and Harvard and Yale, than because we are impelled to our course by an instinctive mental affiliation with the impulses behind the older art and with the cultural and educational principles for which they stand.

I want to emphasize this point very fully: the Gothic restoration is neither a fad nor a case of stylistic predilections. Of course, we like it better than any of the others to which we have any shadow of right, and we think it better art than anything the Renaissance ever produced; but back of this is either a clear conviction or a dim instinct (one is as good as the other as an incentive) that the power that expressed itself through Gothic forms was a saner and more wholesome and altogether nobler thing than that which expressed itself through the art of the Renaissance and all that has succeeded it. In other words, the world is coming to realize something of the significances of art, and its import as human language, not spoken, — for the audible tongue has its own function of expressing mental concepts, — but conveying its message symbolically, and to the imagination, the intuition — if you like, to the soul.

In a way it is all a part of a great revolution, or restoration, that is even now taking place, and is far more significant than many of the more conspicuous and loudly heralded transformations with which the century is rife, a revolution that was inevitable, that is part of the great rhythm of human life that is the underlying force of history. By some mysterious law this vast vibration seems to divide itself into epochs of about five centuries, during each of which a tendency initiated in the preceding period rises to the surface, submerges its predecessor, lifts on an enormous swell, crests,— and then in its turn breaks down and disappears, giving place to its successor whose inconspicuous beginnings have already been disclosed, though dimly. In this great rhythm there are, of course, periodical nodes which are the points where the ascending wave passes that which is descending, and these nodes come almost exactly at five-hundred-year intervals, before and following the Christian era. To speak only of what has been since that date, we find the years 450 to 550, 950 to 1050, and 1450 to 1550 fraught with enormous significance and containing within their span those sudden and violent activities that spelled at the same time the death of one epoch, the birth of another. Similarly we may assume that at least from 1950 on we, or our descendants, shall confront a revolution of the same nature, during which what we now call "modern civilization" (which may be dated roughly from the fall of Constantinople in 1453) will dissolve and disappear as completely as the Roman Empire vanished at the first node after the birth of Christ, the Carolingian empire at the second, and mediævalism at the third; while what takes its place will be as radically different as happened in each of these historic instances. As I have said before, however, the antecedents of revolution and re-creation run far back of the node itself, and as at the cresting of mediævalism we may find in Abélard and the Albigenses, and veiled even in scholasticism, the seed that was not to germinate for many generations, so now, although the great convulsion may be half a century away, we can, if we look, discover the leaven at work and from its manifestations make some estimate of what it will produce when it is in full operation.

Now this leaven shows itself in many forms, and the revival of Gothic architecture is one of them. It is a wide fellowship, this of the prophets, the path-breakers: if, on the one hand, we find, as we should expect, close kin in all the arts, from the nineteenth-century Romanticists in literature and the Pre-Raphaelites and the artist-craftsmen of Morris's following, and

Richard Wagner, down to the horde of lesser lights to-day in literature and painting and music who have broken away from the classical-agnostic type of the latter part of the last century and are returning to the Catholic Middle Ages for their inspiration and their models, so, on the other, do we find an infinity of movements of similar impulse but in far-sundered fields: socialism, for instance, which is a rather insecure and blundering revolt against the whole economic theory and material practice of the last epoch of history; the monastic revival, one of the most significant and amazing episodes of the present day, ignored by the world, yet forging onward year after year with a vitality matched only in the seventh, the twelfth, and the seventeenth centuries; radicalism in politics which, however stupid it may be in its passionate panaceas, is still a real mediæval revolt against the impossible governmental system engendered in the centuries between the Renaissance and our own; the new literature of spiritual dynamics with Chesterton and Hilaire Belloc at the head, battling gloriously against the paynim in the shape of Bennett, Wells, and their kind;

the new-old religious propaganda of such men as Fr. Figgis, Fr. Waggett, the Abbot of Caldey, and Fr. McNabb, withering with its prophetic breath the plausible and ingenious heresies of a Campbell, a Canon Henson, and a Mrs. Eddy; finally, — though there is much unnamed before, — the new philosophy, James, Eucken, Bergson, — the last the greatest figure, perhaps, since St. Thomas Aquinas.

A varied list, is it not? And much still remains unspecified; but it all hangs together; it is all part of a great movement; and the most interesting thing is the fact that it all happens synchronously with the very culmination of its antithesis, the thing it is destined to destroy, the apotheosis of that materialism that is the essence of the epoch now closing in triumphant glory, in war and anarchy, and in the desperation of unrevealed but inevitable defeat.

And here is a point worth noting and that may be made useful. To-day we are surrounded by a very cyclone of reform: from the four winds of heaven we are battered and tempest-tossed by hurtling reforms that leave us no peace and — it must be confessed — afford us scant benefit. We seize them all, we are voracious for reforms, we accept them at their face value, and —again to change the simile—wolf them down like one o'clock. The result is usually unfortunate, for as a matter of fact all is not reform that revolutionizes. There are two kinds of reform, the first that is protective, preventive: reactions engendered by a dying force to save itself, tangents springing from a falling curve and striving to arrest the inevitable descent; the second that engenders tangents that leap upward from the ascending curve, each one of which actually lifts the curve more lightly into the air. At this moment the descending and ascending curves cross, the tangential reactions are very much mixed, and no wonder helpless humanity is confused. But it all becomes clear if we can segregate them in their proper categories. Half the so-called reforms of to-day, and those most loudly acclaimed and avidly accepted, are really no more than the desperate efforts of a dying force to prolong for an hour its pitiful existence, to postpone for a day its inevitable plunge into the sea of oblivion. On the other hand, the other half,—who shall estimate its vast significance, its illimitable dynamic force? Under its varied forms lie the promise and potency of a new era, a new epoch of civilization; and I honestly think the great question that confronts every man to-day, and that must be promptly answered is "On which wave are you riding?" If on that whose crest loomed in the immediate past, then you are riding down the swift glissade of dissolution and your day is nearly done; if on that which only lately has risen out of the dark, then before you lifts an ascent that cannot be checked and whose cresting is perhaps two or three centuries ahead. And in choosing your wave, the isolation of reforms in the two categories I have named will be of assistance towards the determination; for, once accomplished, you will see how many of those alluring panaceas that promise well are but the eloquence of a patent medicine circular, are but dregs and ashes, while things you had little noted, or noted with amused contempt, are actually those centres of vitality, of dynamic force, that are at the same time the guaranty of the termination of a dynasty become corrupt and festering, and of the initiation of another that shall be strong with new and crescent life.

You see? I told you the word "Gothic" would lead me far: farther than you asked, or will like, or will agree to; but to some of us it is like an oriflamme, a standard set up by the king for the rallying of loyalty: the fiery cross of Constantine with its prophetic legend, "By this sign conquer!" Whether we know it or not, — and some of us act by instinct rather than conviction, — we are fighting the battles of a new civilization, which, like all true civilization, is also the old. And it is for this very reason that, unlike our forbears of the beginnings of the crusade, we cannot urge our Gothic as either a universal style, fitted for all conceivable purposes, or as a final thing which consists in the restoration and perpetuation of a mode of art sufficiently determined in the Middle Ages, as Greek, for example, was determined in the Hellenic epoch. Let me say a word on these two points.

The argument — one might almost say the passionate prayer — for a "National Style" is based on an insufficient apprehension of the premises. A national style implies unity of civilization, such, for instance, as happened in the fourth century B.C., the fourth century A.D. in the Eastern Empire, or the thirteenth century throughout Christian Europe: such a condition does not exist to-day — is as far from existence as then it was near. This twentieth century is like a salad dressing: composed of two opposite ingredients which, nevertheless, assembled in unstable equilibrium, produce a most interesting and even useful condiment. On the one hand, we have all the amazing precedents of the last four centuries, from materialism, intellectualism, atheism, and democracy to "big business," syndicalism, and "Votes for Women"; on the other, we have an inheritance from alien and far-distant times: the Home (as distinguished from the uptown flat), the School (when it has not surrendered to manual, vocational, and business training), and the Church, in its ancient aspect, untouched by rationalism, the social club idea, and emotional insanity. There are infinite ramifications of each branch, but the branches are distinct, and like a trunk grafted with apples and roses (I believe this may be done), the flowers are different, and the fruit. Now, as I have said before (and as my hour prolongs itself more strenuously maintain), art is expressive, the highest voicing of the highest things, and if it has two opposites to make manifest it must be true to each and express them in different ways. I do not know what may be the exact and perfect architectural expressions of Wall Street, yellow journalism, commercial colleges, the Structural Steel Union, Christian Science, and equal suffrage: I dare say they are, or may be made, as beautiful as Hellenic or Byzantine or Buddhist architecture; but I am reasonably sure they are not like any of these, and I am firmly persuaded that they cannot be Gothic in any form. On the other hand, as I think I have said before, I am equally sure that a Christian home, a conscientious and high-minded university, and the Catholic Faith are not to be put forward in the sight of men clothed in the Rococo raiment of a Medici-Borgia masquerade or the quaint habiliments of the École des Beaux Arts.

"Every man to his taste," and to each category of human activity its own stylistic expression, for each has its own and nothing is gained by a confusion of categories. Because, we will say, the art of Imperial Rome best expresses the spirit and the function of a metropolitan railway station, it does not follow that it must also be used for the library of a great university; because the soul of the École des Beaux Arts as made manifest through the apartment houses of the Boulevard Raspail, must also inspire the material form of the town house of a "Captain of Industry," it need not inevitably perform the same function in the case of a cathedral; because Gothic of some sort or other best reveals the lineage, the impulse, and the law of an Episcopal parish church, we are not compelled to postulate it for a stock exchange or a department store. In fact, the very reverse is true in all these instances, and those who are most zealous in urging the cause of Gothic for church and school and home are also most jealous of its employment elsewhere; for they know that only those elements in modern civilization which still retain something of the spirit that informed their immediate forbears in the Middle Ages have any right to the forms that spirit created for its own self-expression.

And now, just a word as to these forms themselves, lest you should think, as others have, that the Gothic restoration aims not only at universal sovereignty, but that it is content as well with the restoration as such, aiming to bring back in all its integrity both a dead civilization and its forms. Such an idea would be far from the facts; it is true that at present those that are engaged in the Gothic restoration seldom diverge very far from historical methods and forms. Perhaps the late J. D. Sedding, and George Scott, architect for Liverpool Cathedral, and Leonard Stokes, sometime president of the Royal Institute, diverge farther in this direction; but even they venture but a little way into untrodden paths, while the great majority of practitioners, such as the late George Bodley in England, and Vaughan in America, adhere very closely, indeed, to what has been, adapting it rather than transforming it. This is not because there is anything sacrosanct in these forms and methods, it is not because, as individuals, the men I have named lack either inspiration or power of invention; it is simply because, in the first place, they know that man must not only destroy but restore before he can rebuild, and, in the second place, because they lack the great push behind them of a popular uprising, the incentive of a universal demand, which alone can make individualism creative rather than destructive, dynamic rather than anarchical. This is a fact that is frequently forgotten in categories of activity other than those purely æsthetic, and if in economics, politics, and philosophy men would realize its truth, we should less often be threatened by plausible reforms that are actually deformatory in their character. However this may be, it is certainly so in architecture, and, therefore, we are content at present to restore; for we know that by so doing not only do we regain a body of laws, precedents, and forms that are the only foundation for the superstructure of which we dream, but also because through these very qualities we may, in a measure, establish and make operative again, by analogy and suggestion, those stimuli that in time may react on society itself, transforming it into a new estate, when man will enter into the new spiritual life which will demand a creative and revealing art, such as that of the Middle Ages, and in accordance with law this demand will guarantee the supply.

For art of all sorts is not only expressive, it is also creative: if it is in one sense the flower of a civilization, it is in another the fruit, and in its burgeoning lies also the promise of a new life after the winter of the declining curve is past and the new line begins its ascending course. Bad art — for there is such, though it is a contradiction in terms—works powerfully for bad living and bad thinking, while, on the other hand, good art is in its very nature regenerative and beneficent. It cannot save the age of which it is the flower from inevitable decay, but, even as the treasures of classical civilization were preserved in the monasteries of the Dark Ages until better days, so does it lie fallow for generations only to rise again into the light for the inception of a new civilization.

This, then, is the significance of the contemporary Gothic restoration, and we who believe in it, who give it our most earnest support, do so less as artists than as missionaries, confident that if we can bring it back, even at first on the old lines, we shall have been working in the service of humanity.

Shall we rest there? Shall we restore a style, and a way of life, and a mode of thought? Shall we re-create an amorphous mediævalism and live listlessly in that fool's paradise? On the contrary. When a man finds himself confronting a narrow stream, with no bridge in sight, does he leap convulsively on the very brink and then project himself into space? If he does he is very apt to fail of his immediate object, which is to get across. No; he retraces his steps, gains his running start, and clears the obstacle at a bound. This is what we architects are doing when we fall back on the great past for our inspiration; this is what, specifically, the Gothicists are particularly doing. We are getting our running start, we are retracing our steps to the great Christian Middle Ages, not that there we may remain, but that we may achieve an adequate point of departure; what follows must take care of itself.

And, by your leave, in following this course

we are not alone, we have life with us; for at last life also is going backward, back to gather up the golden apples lost in the wild race for prizes of another sort, back for its running start, that it may clear the crevasse that startlingly has opened before it. Beyond this chasm lies a new field, and a fair field, and it is ours if we will. The night has darkened, but lightened toward dawn; there is silver on the edges of the hills and promise of a new day, not only for architects, but for every man.

III

THE PLACE OF THE FINE ARTS IN PUBLIC EDUCATION

III

THE PLACE OF THE FINE ARTS IN PUBLIC EDUCATION [1]

AS the strange madness we call the Renaissance prevailed increasingly over Europe, blotting out the last faint flickerings of that artistic fire that had been a lamp to the feet of innumerable generations, and substituting therefor the pale *ignis-fatuus* of conscious and scholastic artifice, synchronously grew an original and hitherto unheard-of theory of the nature and function of the fine arts, carrying with it the novel and alien idea of concrete, specific, premeditated "art education." A new thing, indeed, as though one should establish schools of gastronomy, lectureships on the art of sleep, academies of inhalation and exhalation. Novel, yes; but imperative both then and now, owing necessity, however, not to a more liberal and enlightened conception of art in itself, but

1 Read at Commencement, Yale University School of Fine Arts.

rather to the ominous and most unwholesome revolution that, in the tempest of change, had hurled from their enduring pedestals the proven laws of life, substituting in their place the brazen images of a dumb idolatry; robbing man of his divine birthright in beauty, the heritage of ages unnumbered, the indelible mark and token of God in His world.

When the great epoch of paganism crumbled and sunk into dust and ashes, tried and found wanting by the touchstone of divine revelation, St. Benedict was raised up for the founding of a new institution, based on the stern rejection of the dearest privileges of man, but, because of this very rejection and denial, competent to meet in the highest degree the desperate needs of a racked and shattered era. But for the monks in their hidden monasteries, the very seed of civilization would have perished from the earth; and so we may say with equal truth that, however false the new view of art, however unwholesome the new idea of premeditated art education, but for these same schools of art, from the days of the Medici until now, the world would have lost that which was even of greater value than the Greek and Roman manuscripts and the dim traditions of perished glory, that lay for centuries in monkish cloisters and in monkish hearts.

But the pious conserving of shards and shreds is not all, and with the mediæval monks in their first estate, we have sometimes been content with such conservation, forgetting that something lies behind, and that, the inner meaning of the stores in our treasure-house; their function, their message, their significance.

Nothing else, indeed, would have been possible, for with the Renaissance came into the world a new theory of art: and this was that, instead of being what it is, the touchstone of civilization, it was simply an amenity of life, a conscious product, and a marketable commodity. This novel idea has persisted until to-day, and the result is that the real nature of art has remained forgotten, and in spite of the protests of the artist and of the teacher, we have persisted in regarding our art schools much as we do our "commercial colleges" and our schools of applied science; that is, as agencies of specialization maintained for the benefit of those who, by their mental temper, are biased in favour of architecture or painting or the industrial arts, on the one hand, or of bookkeeping, stenography, mechanical engineering, on the other. This is to miss the entire significance of art and to relegate it to a position where it is meaningless, impotent, dead. We study Greek and Latin, history, literature, philosophy, mathematics, not, primarily, that we may become specialists in the use of one or the other, at a given rate of pecuniary compensation, but that we may become cultivated men, and this should be our attitude toward the fine arts; for the day is not far distant when the school of art will be, not an accessory or an adjunct to a university, as is the school of mines or the dental school, but as absolutely and intimately a part of its prescribed curriculum as the ancient languages or philosophy or letters.

Art is, I repeat, neither an industry nor a product; it is a mystery, a manifestation, and a result. Through it alone we come face to face with the spiritual output of the racial soul, through it is revealed all that endures in civilization. I claim for it, therefore, a coördinate position with all other branches of learning, as indispensable in a complete curriculum, since it is at the same time inerrant as a record of achievement, inspiring toward effective action to a degree unmatched in other categories, and finally, a great language for the voicing of the greatest things, a language for which there is no substitute, and he who is not learned therein, either in its active or its passive aspect, is to that extent ignorant, unlearned, uncultured.

Art is the revelation of the human soul, not a by-product of industrialism.

During the great period of Christian civilization, this truth was held universally; not consciously, of course, nor as the outcome of a scientific demonstration; the Christian centuries worked after another method. To the sane men of mediævalism there were two categories of phenomena: axioms and mysteries; and the frontiers of the two domains were fixed and final. Very fortunately for the future, the mysteries were themselves held to be axiomatic, and so long as this was true a just balance existed in life. It was not until the daimon of a haunting paganism rose from the tomb of a dead past, bringing the bright fruit of the tree of knowledge in its hands, and on its lips the words the serpent had said before, "Eat thereof, then your eyes shall be opened and ye shall be as gods, knowing good and evil," — it was not until then, the fruit eaten, that man swelled in pride and said, "Behold, there is no mystery," and the victory of the Renaissance was accomplished.

As the nineteenth century takes its place in history, we obtain a certain effect of perspective and we see how wholly it was meshed in that web of futility and error, "There is no mystery." Truly, to us of the new century it begins to seem that nothing else rightly exists. At all events, we realize that the things of worth and moment are the mysteries; the things of indifference the demonstrable facts. So mediævalism held art; a thing universal and inevitable; inseparable from life and bound up in the being of every man; but a thing so potent, so sovereign, and in its effects so disproportioned to its palpable means, that it became one with all the other inexplicable potencies — a mystery.

Now, it is a curious fact that when we come to understand a thing finally and explicitly, we are unable to use it to our spiritual advantage, or to the ultimate welfare of the race. Here lies the most serious stigma upon the last century, which was so given over to the inordinate manufacturing of the most exquisite and technically faultless theories, devices, and machines for the production of quite useless institutions and commodities. The phenomenon we accept but cannot comprehend; the looming wonder that compels us but eludes hand and brain forever; — this is the momentous thing, the driving impulse of all that splendid spiritual and intellectual activity that, through its immortal products, endures eternally as the ever-growing heritage of man. Where knowledge ceases, mystery begins, and the better part of man never emerges from those cloud confines where amid the lightning and the tempest God is seen face to face; that magical castle of cloud and mist across whose dim portals the rainbow writes, "Knowledge abandon, ye who enter here."

This revelation of the eternal, impassable

limitation of human knowledge, combined with that other which is its perfect compensation, the doctrine that all things are sacramental, possessing an "inward and spiritual grace" that is apprehended through the "outward and visible sign," was and is the essential element in Christianity which made it victor over the paganism that believed all things were possible to the human mind. So mediævalism held, and holding brought into being St. Thomas Aquinas and St. Francis, Dante and Giotto and Fra Angelico; the cathedral builders of France and the abbey builders of England. For the two essential truths in the world are religion and art, and these two are mysteries; rationalize them and they cease, for their motive power is gone. Of this rationalizing, of this Pandora's quest for the facts in the case, there was nothing, and, therefore, misled in no degree as to the supposed existence of a science either of religion or of art, mediævalism raised both to the highest point yet attained by man.

With the outbreak of the Renaissance came the catastrophe, for behind the recrudescent pagan forms, behind the cry of humanism and emancipation, lay the old pagan theory that to human reason all things are possible. Mystery was abolished by edict, and the "light of pure reason" took its place, though three centuries and more were necessary wholly to effect the substitution. Little by little the Renaissance modulated into the Reformation, and this in its turn merged in the Revolution. Each of these several aspects of one primary impulse played its own necessary part in the great breaking-up of the just and well-balanced order Christianity had brought into being. The Renaissance of Borgia and Medici destroyed the whole system of natural morality and made for the moment the Church herself a stench to the nostrils and a scandal. The Protestantism of Luther and Calvin, frantic against the flagrant immorality raging like a pestilence around the very throne of St. Peter, turned, the ethical regeneration inaugurated, into a propaganda for the substitution, in place of the wonder and the mysticism of the Catholic Faith, of hard, mechanical, logical, and literal dogmas; easily framed in words, clearly demonstrable to the most cloudy mental faculties. Finally, the Revolution came to deny everything: Catholic, Renaissance, Protestant alike; law and order, obedience, honour, even the palpable decencies of life; one thing only it did not deny, the basic principle of the Renaissance, "There is no mystery." Then the Revolution passed like a paralyzing nightmare, leaving the field swept clear of all that Christianity had brought into existence, and since then we have been permitted year by year to watch the unshackled, untrammelled mind struggling to build a new heaven and a new earth over the ruins of the old.

Now the reaction comes, and the gray dawn that glimmered fitfully through the storm wrack of the nineteenth century brightens to another day. The light falls on every domain of life, shining through the still buffeting storm; on industry, economics, philosophy, ethics, politics, education, letters, religion; but nowhere does it lie with a kindlier radiance than on the great domain of art. It is not alone that once more man clamours for beauty and its ministry, and men rise up to answer the demand in kind: beyond this lies the fact that the old dogmas no longer hold; and the question goes forth, "What is art, what does it signify, what are the laws of its causation?" Everywhere men are searching the answer, poring over the art records of the past that the great cataclysm has left us, comparing them with the times that brought them forth, testing these times again by the spirit that led them, building up by slow degrees a new biology that is in very fact the science of civilization.

In the process strange things are revealed; no longer bound by inherited prejudice, and not wholly in bondage now to the intellectual superstitions of the period of modern enlightenment, while acquiring a measure of Christian humility in the matter of the omnipotence of mentality, we go back to the original records, draw our own independent inferences, and, comparing these with long accepted authorities, discover that the deductions and conclusions that served for past generations satisfy us no longer. Are we right in thinking it all a system of specious special pleading, this mass of august testimony to the essential barbarism of Christian civilization and to the essential glory of the threefold epoch that took its place? To such a new conclusion we tend beyond a doubt; and while we still admit the great necessity of many post-mediæval principles and motives, we are coming to believe that these developed through the Renaissance, the Reformation, and the Revolution, not by reason of them; while each has left us, on the other hand, a heritage of evil to the extinction of which the present century is consecrated.

It would be a facile task and fascinating to examine, one by one, the several categories of contemporary spiritual, mental, and physical activity, pointing out in each how the evil aspects, that force themselves on us with such insistency to-day, hark back inevitably to one or the other of the three allied dominations that controlled the destinies of the world from the exile of the Popes at Avignon to the battle of Waterloo. It is sufficient for the moment for us to deal only with the question of the fine arts, since my object in speaking to you is to draw your attention to certain aspects of the question of the place the study of the philosophy and history of art should have in the scheme of liberal education.

Before all else, however, we must disabuse our minds of that idea of the nature of art which has maintained itself so firmly during the last four centuries. Art is not a possibly desirable amenity of life, to be acquired as a gloss to a commercial and industrial supremacy; neither is it a series of highly specialized professions. Art is a result, not a product; and it is also a language. Given a certain degree of individual or racial or national civilization and the inevitable reaction is art in the abstract. The demand for expression is instant and, under the same civilized conditions, the manifestation is immediate and instinctive, and this is art in the concrete. Art is, therefore, a language, but it deals with emotions, concepts, and impulses that cannot be expressed through any other medium known to man, because these emotions, concepts, and impulses are the highest, and therefore the most mysterious and tenuous, of which the soul has cognition. "There is a physical body and a spiritual body"; and so also there is a physical mind and a spiritual mind. The former deals with all that lies between the cradle and the grave, the latter with the treasured consciousness of the innumerable æons of life that preceded this little hour of earthly habitation, and with the innumerable æons that shall succeed. Natural science is the concrete manifestation of the first, religion of the second, and art in all its forms is the perfect manifestation of this spiritual mind, as the written and spoken language is the voicing of the physical mind until, indeed, it takes upon itself symbolical quality, when it becomes one with the fine arts and consecrated to other service.

Art, then, is language and its mode is symbolism, and the thing that lies behind is the essential man in his highest estate.

As we became more and more ignorant of the very meaning of the word, we, as children of the Renaissance, slowly and arduously evolved the nineteenth-century theory of art which, even more than the Renaissance and the Reformation, was instrumental in stamping out the last smouldering embers of the thing itself. Where once art had been as natural and inevitable an attribute of man as religion or love or war or children, it now found itself an exotic, an appanage of the elect few, a thing too tenuous and aloof for common humanity. Such a theory as this means simply the extinction of art, which cannot live in the thin air of Brahminical exclusiveness; it is the exact, the instant, and the complete language of man in his spiritual experiences; and while to only one in a thousand is it given now, or ever was given, to become a creative artist, behind such a one lies the clamouring world of men, and it is this that manifests itself through his art, not his own solitary soul. If, like Phidias, Sophocles, Dante, Giotto, Shakespeare, Wagner, Browning, he is a true and faithful interpreter of the best, the race answers instantly, unless it has lost or stultified this sixth and highest sense, as has happened in history only in modern times. To bring back this marvellous gift of God to a hungry generation, to win again the old lamps foolishly bartered for new, — the old lamps that, at a touch, brought genii and afrits and all the magical spirits of fire and air to the service of the summoner, — this is the task before us. And the labour is not, as the amateurs and savants and literati of the Renaissance, or the æsthetes of the nineteenth-century decadence would have held, because it is a polite accomplishment and a facile means of class distinction, but because it is the immutable mark of civilization, the infallible touchstone of human achievement. Art means civilization, the lack of it barbarism, and year by year, in spite of splendid sporadic manifestations, this lack has become ever more and more marked since the middle of the fourteenth century, when the old lamps were sold for the new.

Now, it is quite clear that to endeavour to foster the passion for beauty and the instinct for art, by the deliberate and scientific methods that have held for some five centuries, is to continue our self-indulgence in the vain repetition of history. By taking thought we cannot add one cubit to our stature, devise a new religion (though of late some have thought otherwise), or re-create art. We can do many things, but none of these. Art is the result of certain conditions: bring these into being, and you cannot escape great art; eliminate them, and no power on earth can make art live. For five centuries we have been bending all our energies toward the extinction of these conditions, and the success that has followed has been very considerable. If we desire a vital art we must reverse our policy. Art cannot exist side by side with atheism, agnosticism, or infidelity; it is impossible in conjunction with our contemporary conception of what constitutes democracy: it dies before defiance of law and order and denial of the principle of subservience to authority; before the individualism of the nineteenth century and contemporary standards of caste; it is trampled to death in the economic and industrial Armageddon that surges over the stricken field of contemporary life. In a word, the evils of the Renaissance-Reformation-Revolution, which for the moment are somewhat more conspicuous in their activity than the virtues, are the negation of art-producing conditions.

We may put to one side the thought of a conscious propaganda for the restoration of art, devoting ourselves to the achievement of art-producing conditions, the solving of the religious, governmental, economic, industrial, and social problems that confront us, like the solid ranks of a conquering army. If we solve them aright, art follows as the guerdon of victory.

And here emerges from the mist of theory the new doctrine of the importance of the fine arts in every scheme of liberal education. I am not speaking now of the creative artist or of the manner of his education; indeed, I am not sure that to him education is a necessity, or that by such methods can he be created. He will occur, however unfavourable the conditions or inclement and forbidding the time. The question before us is the place of the fine arts in *general* education, in their function as contributors to the making of a well-founded man. Now, in the process of development, we have reached a point where we no longer sound the tocsin, plant the standard of battle, build barricades in city streets, and go forth killing and, if it may be, to conquer. We have another way, we teach; substituting education for coercion, and until the event dethrones our theory, we shall believe the way a better one, and that by our schools and colleges and universities we shall build such character as will restore those just and wholesome conditions that will express themselves through that great pæan of joy and exultation and worship we call art.

There are certain schemes of education that tend inevitably to this end; there are others that work as inevitably against it. Art-producing civilization is engendered by educational systems that are conceived on the lines of eternal truth, not on those of time-serving expediency. During the nineteenth century a new theory came into vogue, the theory, novel and without recognizable ancestry, that the object of education is the breeding of specialists, whether they be dental surgeons or bacteriologists, bankers, or veterinarians; and that, to this end, everything not conspicuously contributory to intensified specialization should be eliminated; that the years given to education should be shortened, and again shortened, in order that a man might the sooner hurl himself into the struggle for life. From this point of view everything not obviously practical was discredited: Latin and Greek became matters of indifference when an electrician or a financier was in the making; the history of civilization, the development of organized religion, comparative literature, philosophy, were eliminated from the education of the architect and the engineer. That the result was a great body of men of unbalanced intellect and very flimsy culture is, I think, a statement that may be defended, and the present century, even in its extreme youth, gives evidence of a radical revolt from the once popular standards of its predecessor. A new principle has come, — or rather an old principle has been restored; and we confront the definite dogma that specialization is almost wholly a matter for post-graduate education, while the object of the school and the college and the university is above all else the development of gentlemen of well-rounded personalities, who, grounded and fixed in all that pertains to general culture, rendered conversant with all the civilization of the past and its monuments, trained and disciplined in all that pertains to intellectual and spiritual experience, may be prepared for entering at a later time into that course of specialization which is imperative and inevitable.

Professor William James has of late shown very clearly the questionable results, in the domain of pure science, of a system of education too highly specialized and too contemptuous of other fields of mental and spiritual activity; and already a movement has begun amongst architects and engineers — two of the most highly specialized of professions — in favour of a scheme of training which shall extend over a far longer term of years and be devoted, for the major part of this period, to the assimilation of those elements of pure culture which apparently, and in the nineteenth-century view, have no direct bearing on the case, but tend only toward the goal of general cultivation.

The old system of electives, specialization, and short-term training has brought us to a debatable pass; our civilization is menaced by strange and ominous tendencies and impulses; if we are to stem the tide of crescent barbarism, which in spite of our vast and penetrating educational organism has risen up against us, we must follow, not the nineteenth but the twentieth century in its educational tendencies. And so following, we shall find that it is not a question of conservation that confronts us, but of extension, of the acceptance of new or long-forgotten agencies toward the development of pure culture, and of these none quite stands on the level of the history and theory and philosophy of the fine arts. Abandoning forever the idea of the arts as a product, and accepting them as a manifestation, we shall soon realize that without a full familiarity with their history and of the philosophy of their being, liberal education is an impossibility. These things can no more be omitted from the education of the prospective merchant and financier and scientist than from that of the professional educator; for they are the basis of culture, and without culture we are barbarians, however much the balance of trade may be in our favour at the end of any given fiscal year.

And of all these great educational agencies I place at the head, art, in its history, its philosophy, its practice; for it is the summing-up of all that goes before: the true history of the true man; and its records are infinitely more reliable and significant than are those chronicles that concern themselves with the unimportant details of the rise and fall of dynasties, the fabrication and annulment of laws, the doings and death of kings. The Middle Ages are inexplicable unless you read their revelation in Chartres and Amiens and Paris and Westminster and Wells, and in the shattered vestiges of monastic glory that cast their wistful glamour over the English counties while they blot a nation's history with the enduring annals of a stupendous crime. The Renaissance is an impossible interlude of horror, dissociated from the splendid vesture the painters and sculptors and poets wrought out of the inheritance of mediævalism to clothe its pagan nakedness. And why? Simply because through art alone has been expressed those qualities which reach above the earth-circle, those things which are the essential elements of the race and time.

For art is the voicing of the oversoul, the manifestation of the superman, and through art alone can we read of essential things. Monasticism, the crusades, feudalism, chivalry are to us matters aloof and incredible, but they brought into being an art that rises even higher than the art of Greece; and through study of this art we are able to see into the soul of the time-spirit that created it, and, so seeing, we are no longer able to call the great institutions of mediævalism barbarous and darkened, for their real nature is revealed, and we know them for what they were, foundation stones of civilization.

For many generations we have been taught to look on the Dark Ages, mediævalism, the Renaissance, the Reformation, the Revolution, from certain definite standpoints. We have been led to believe that with the climax of the Middle Ages, the great epoch associated with the names of Greece and Rome, which had slowly crumbled after Rome herself had received her deathblow at the hands of Northern barbarians, had, in its long-continued degeneration, reached at last its pit of final fall, whence it has been steadily emerging by virtue of the impulse imparted by the Renaissance, established by the Reformation, and guaranteed by the Revolution, until at last it has mounted to the dizzy height where now it stands poised for further flight. Now this theory, so simple, so cheerful and gratifying, is challenged; men are not wanting to declare the Middle Ages to be one of the starlike points of man's achievement, the Renaissance but the first aspect of a great catastrophe that was to overwhelm Christian civilization in ruin. Now, even if this theory is extreme and but the natural revulsion of feeling sequent on the sudden discovery of a false path followed too long, it is still true that the present estimate of the Renaissance is quite as different from the old as is the new view of mediævalism. For this radical and most salutary change we are indebted in a great degree to the rediscovery of the fine arts that occurred in the last century, and to the resulting conviction that through them we might scrutinize the history of the times that employed them, to our own advantage and to the extreme benefit of our historical perspective. Already through our study of mediæval art we have come to learn something of what mediævalism really was, and now we are applying the same test to the Renaissance; though with a difference, for here we have forgiven Alexander VI and Leo X, Torquemada and Machiavelli, for the sake of Leonardo, Botticelli, Donatello, and Mino da Fiesole, whereas, when we come to study the philosophy of the art of the Renaissance, we find that the major part of it was, not the fruit of the "Revival of Learning," but in simple fact the very flowering of mediævalism; acquiring little from the Renaissance beyond certain accidents of form, the soul remaining mediæval still. Shorn of the great names of the cinquecento, and with little left of artistic glory save the transitionals (Michelangelo, Raphael, Cellini), the Renaissance seems gaunt enough, for its true artistic expression appears in such doleful form as Guido, the Caracci, Salvator Rosa, and the so-called "architects" of Roman grandiosity. Here are two examples of the radical change in our view of comparative civilization that has been effected through the study and appreciation of art; and if a third is needed, witness Japan, where, through art appreciation, our eyes became opened to the existence of a great and wonderful civilization unparallelled, almost, in its intensity and its enduring nature.

But it is not only as the test of history, the measure of comparative civilization, that the study and appreciation of art in all its forms is of inestimable value. Above all this, it is the touchstone of life, the prover of standards, the director of choice. Accepted, assimilated, it becomes one of the great builders of character, linked indissolubly with religion and philosophy toward the final goal of right feeling, right thinking, and right conduct. The false principles of the sixteeeth century, the savage hatred of the seventeenth, the chaos and violence on the one hand and the empty formalism on the other, of the eighteenth, the materialism and the mental self-satisfaction of the nineteenth century, all worked together to crush out of humanity this greatest gift of God; but the revulsion has come, the fruit of the tree of knowledge has been eaten and it is very bitter, and once more men rise up to proclaim the existence and the glory of the unsolvable mysteries, and to demand again their heritage in beauty and art.

For from the beginning of things beauty has been the last resort of man when he has risen above his earthly limitations and has laid hold on immortality. In Eastern philosophy we read of karma, that essential thing that persists through death and beyond dissolution, linking life to life in an endless sequence of change and evolution; and whether, with the East, we believe this golden chain to be woven of myriads of sequent lives that are yet one, or whether, with the West, we hold it to be but the persisting inheritance from equal myriads of ancestors, the thing itself we accept, and art, itself a sacrament, shows through the outward and visible sign, which is beauty, the inward and spiritual grace that is built up of sequent lives and combined experiences.

Beauty is a mystery, for it is a great symbol. Why, we do not know, but the fact is there. Out of the accumulated approximations to infinity that have marked ten thousand thousand forgotten lives, we have reared a Great Approximation, which may be called the Intimation of the Absolute, and beauty is the mode of its manifestation, art the concrete expression thereof. Regarded in this light and not as a group of specialized activities, we see at once how absolutely it becomes a part of a liberal education, perhaps even the highest part. In themselves the facts of date and method and authorship are secondary and unimportant when we study the cathedrals of France, the abbeys of England, the sculpture of Greece and that of thirteenth-century Europe and of Fujiwara Japan, the Gregorian music of Italy and the nineteenth-century music of Germany, the painting of the Italian cinquecento, and of the Hangchou epoch in China and the Ashikaga period in Japan. These are but the documents in the case, the data furnished us by generations unnumbered; and through them, by the processes of pure philosophy, we may lay hold of that which we cannot acquire through any other means whatever — the spiritual experiences and the spiritual achievements of dead civilizations.

And this is history, its acquisition and assimilation, culture. Dynastic facts, material products, the historical kaleidoscope of changing laws and customs, ecclesiastical councils, fluctuant heresies and defiant counter-reformations, — what are these but the dry bones religion and art make beautiful and alive? The art of a time is the touchstone of its efficiency and by that art shall it be judged. And more: through study of the philosophy of beauty and through a recognition of what art signifies of any race or time, we shall come to that revision of standards which is the inevitable precursor of a new epoch of civilization. Neither socialism nor public-school education, secularism nor ethical culture, free silver nor the strenuous life, can serve as antidote to the ills that confront us; but only that fundamental revision of standards that will show us the true inwardness of the trust and the labour union, the professional politician and the grafter, the money test of social distinctions, and contemporary newspaper journalism. By acceptance of the artistic tests, and by proficiency in that philosophy of art which makes the application of these tests possible, we are put in possession of a kind of universal solvent, a final common denominator, and before our eyes the baffling chaos of chronicles, records, and historic facts opens out into order and simplicity; for the facts in the case prove only what was *done*, the art testimony reveals what was thought and felt and imagined — in other words, *why* the things were done.

And so we return to our original proposition: the statement that the Renaissance brought into being a theory of art categorically false and inevitably destructive of that which it strove to patronize. To do this, to foist this profound and far-reaching heresy on the world, it had first to destroy the sound and lucid view of art that had been inherited from paganism by Christianity and maintained intact until the fifteenth century. The time has come at last for a return to the ancient ideals, for the falsity of the substitute has proved itself; and to effect this end the first thing we have to do is to admit that beauty is one of the sacraments in a universe wholly and absolutely sacramental in its nature; the second is to realize that this same sacrament of beauty is the symbolical expression of the experiences and the achievements of the human soul; and the third is to reject the Renaissance idea that art is an affair of caste as already we have rejected the Protestant idea that it is a snare of the devil, recognizing it, as in truth it is, the evidence of true civilization and its only unerring record.

Then follows the new building-up; the study and formulating of the philosophy of art as a result, a manifestation, and a language. And in the process greater things will follow than a revision of our historical estimates, than a new vision of the essential things in human life. We shall, I believe, change our attitude toward the great thousand years of Christian domination, toward the Renaissance and the several modifications thereof which we know beneath a different nomenclature. It is conceivable, also, that our estimate of the nineteenth century itself may be modified in certain particulars; but, however desirable these changes may be, and to me it seems that their importance can hardly be estimated in words, there is yet another thing that will follow, of importance paramount and inestimable, and that is the great revision of standards, the reëstablishing of that proper sense of proportion that alone can guarantee the continuation and the onward development of civilization itself.

It has been sometimes said, though without a deep sense of conviction, and certainly without enthusiastic response on the part of the general public, that whatever we have gained through our great eras of the dominion of industrialism and of natural science has been at the expense of a sense of proportion. To me this seems axiomatic, despite its unpopularity.

Scrutinize closely the standards that reveal themselves through contemporary journalism, Pennsylvania politics, San Francisco graft, the Cœur d'Alene affair, the life insurance and railroad and trust investigations, the present protective tariff, the congressional attitude toward pensions, river and harbour improvements, and colonial import duties, the divorce epidemic, Dowieism, Eddyism, Sanfordism; and, contrasting these, as they reveal themselves, with the standards of the monasticism of the Dark Ages, the crusades and the chivalry of mediævalism, answer whether or no "lack of sense of proportion" is not the gentlest term that may be applied to the contemporary spirit of the world.

I began by saying that to me the inalienable rights of man were religion, art, and joyful labour. We have rejected the first, destroyed the latter, and I am willing to defend the thesis that our action in these directions is primarily responsible for the disappearance of the third from life as we know it. How are we to regain our birthright; how reëstablish once more the consciousness of the impassable barrier between the knowable and the unknowable; restore again acceptance of the eternal truth that the seen is but the pale type of the unseen; overthrow the great heresy, "There is no mystery"? how rebuild that essential sense of proportion and of relative values, how effect that revision of standards that must precede a new epoch of civilization? History gives record of but two methods that have been effective in the past; the vast religious revolution and the purging fire of national disaster and barbarian invasion. As for the first, no St. Benedict, St. Bernard, or St. Francis is for the moment visible, but only false prophets of a false dawn; and as for the latter, God forbid that we should await this last resort of divine justice. There is, theoretically speaking, a third way, but one which has, I believe, never yet been essayed with success; still, the chance is there, and, if we are wise, we shall take the chance. From the standpoint of pure reason it would seem possible for us to learn a lesson from the past and so avert that vain repetition of history to which we claim to be averse. And what the real past was, not what it seems through its mere materialization, art most potently helps us to know.

To art men turned when the joy of living and the wonder of spiritual experience and the passion of religious ardour became intolerable in their poignancy and clamorous for perfect expression; to art we must return, that, by its talismanic potency, it may unlock the barred gates of human experience. This also is the primary object of liberal education, and when we have achieved this knowledge, we shall find that the veil is lifted, that our sense of proportion has returned, that our standards are again at one with the standards of all history and need no further revision. Once more we shall find religion and art and joyful labour the restored essentials of life, and then the higher mission of our schools of art will have been accomplished, and our burgeoning civilization will blossom gloriously in the painters and the sculptors and architects, the musicians and poets and craftsmen, who, no longer voices crying in the wilderness, will become the inspired mouthpieces of an emancipated race, proclaiming the wonder and the glory of a noble and a beautiful and a joyful life.

IV

THE ARTIST AND THE WORLD

IV

THE ARTIST AND THE WORLD[1]

FOR two generations we have watched the crescent enthusiasm for art, and the feverish widening of art interest and art activity that are the continuance in a new community of a movement engendered in the Old World, now nearly a century ago. The significance of the movement is profound, its possibilities for good almost unlimited, but its dangers are no less, and it is of these dangers I desire to speak at this time.

I propose to say something as to the relation of the artist to society, to the world of men and women that is at the same time his environment, his inspiration, and his opportunity. Of the artist, whatever one of the seven great arts he follows, — for artistic differentiation is accidental, — the artistic impulse is one.

We hear very much of the relation of the artist to his own particular art, to art itself, to history

[1] Read at Commencement, Yale University School of Fine Arts.

and tradition: I myself have had the honour of speaking in this place on the position art should hold in its relation to education; in season and out of season I have urged the intimate bond that unites art and religion in a common service. With your permission we will broaden the scope of our persistent inquiry, and ask as to the function of the artist as an integral member of that human society which is so much greater and more momentous than he or any other individual; that common life of humanity of which the artist is the product and that he is bound to serve with all the great and singular powers that mark his personality.

It is not inappropriate that such an inquiry should be made in this place and at this time. The Yale School of Fine Arts is not a centre of empirical theorizing, an archæological gymnasium, a laboratory of scientific research; it is a school of artists; it aims to reveal something of the eternal significance of art, to arouse those æsthetic faculties that have lain dormant in our race so many generations, in order that they may become creative agencies, manifesting themselves in time and space for the service of man, and therefore for the glory of God. Such a school I conceive to be the only type that is justifiable, — since schools we must have for the regaining of our lost heritage, — but it is precisely here that perils intrude themselves most insidiously, wherefore they must always be held clearly in mind; for not even religion itself is more endangered by the "false doctrine, heresy, and schism" from which we rightly pray to be delivered.

Do not misunderstand me, I beg of you. I do not dream of postulating of art schools in general, still less of this Yale school in particular, a primacy in error or a peculiarity of sole possession. The dangers lie, not in the schools as such, but in society itself; in the very bone and sinew of man as he is to-day. They are part and parcel of our own contemporary civilization, and they show themselves in Church and in state, in business and professional and social life, more generally, perhaps, than in the life of art; but it is in the latter category that they may be most fatal in their operation. It matters comparatively little if for the moment the Church or some sect abandons itself to evil artistic tendencies; if a combination of illiterate legislators and a temporarily omnipotent politician are victorious in their schemes for defeating the ends of culture and civilization; if the preponderating weight of public opinion degrades the drama, prostitutes music and poetry to the most ignoble ends, and makes of the great art of religious ceremonial a barren desert or a riot of degenerate taste. All these pass; they are the froth of a churning maelstrom of new activity; but if the artist is himself false to the ideal of his art, if he yields to the insidious influences that surround him, then not only is he faithless to the trust imposed in him through the gift of artistic expression, but he engenders a poison that courses subtly and far through the veins of the society he came into the world to serve.

During the last century it is hard to suppose that a true philosophical conception of art should have achieved popular acceptance, and as a matter of fact it did not, the proudest products being similar in their nature to that definition of beauty evolved by Grant Allen: "The æsthetically beautiful is that which affords the maximum of stimulation with the minimum of fatigue or waste, in processes not directly connected with vital functions"; surely the most grotesque example of serene incapacity anywhere recorded in that congeries of incapacities, the literature of æsthetics. It is, however, of great value as putting in concrete form the spiritual inefficiency of the dominant influence in the nineteenth century, and it is just because a new tendency now is visible that we may take heart of hope and believe that a saner and more penetrating view is possible.

As a matter of fact, a profound revolution is now in process, a revolution that is interpenetrating every category of intellectual and spiritual activity, and by the glare of the red conflagrations that are crumbling the tall towers of our intellectual pride, we see revealed the cloud-capped mountains of spiritual endeavour, piercing that very heaven of mystery we with infinite labour had striven to scale with our Babel-towers of misguided ingenuity.

Very slowly it is dawning on us that for several centuries we have been confusing our categories and, by methods and agencies adequate to the estimating of phenomena, have been trying to weigh and determine the Absolute Truth that lies behind and above. Failing miserably, we have come to doubt, not the efficiency of our methods, but the very existence of anything they could not demonstrate. This, I think, is the essence of the great revolution now going on about us, and even more within ourselves: the discovery that those brilliant products of our epoch, natural science and natural philosophy, have their limitations; that beyond the uttermost radius of their possible activity lies the vast and mysterious domain of the real, the Absolute; as vital to man and as unconquered as ever it was in the past; as unconquered, but neither forbidden nor beyond achievement, since by the grace of God even that Absolute, that final mystery of ultimate truth, reveals itself symbolically to those who open their hearts in reverence and with humble spirit, even though it is denied to that insolence of assumed wisdom that presumes to set metes and bounds to the infinite majesty of God.

And it is this high function of superhuman revelation to which I refer when I speak of all art as the natural, and, indeed, the only adequate, expression in time and space of spiritual things. This it has been in all the great past; this it must be in the great future. Adopting this final view of the essential function of art, we shall see, I think, how great the danger that follows from the acceptance of any less lofty view, how incalculable the loss to society, and how much a matter of moment is the question of the relation of the artist to the world of men and women in which he lives, how limitless the field that opens before him, how far-flung and wide-reaching the lines of his service.

Master of the great language, articulate amongst the tongueless, it is for him to express all the spiritual essays, ventures, and discoveries; all the dreams, aspirations, and visions of the mounting wave of humanity that bears him on its crest toward the stars. Seer, spokesman, and prophet, he divines in scientific triumphs the inner significance that gives them value and that the scientist himself sometimes sees not at all; material, industrial, economical development are to him but husks hiding a precious kernel; democracy, socialism, anarchy but the ugly outward form of the enchanted prince in the fairy tale. Through crabbed shards he penetrates to the hidden jewel, snatches it forth, and uplifts it in the sight of wondering men. This he does in his function as seer: as mouthpiece he proclaims the hidden mysteries of the soul, the quests and pilgrimages and adventures of the knights-errant of the spirit; not his own alone,— less his than those of all his fellows, to whom, by some mystical affinity, his consciousness is delicately attuned, answering the faint and distant call, voicing it in the universal language he alone commands, though every God-given soul wholly and instantly comprehends. And as prophet he distances the runners in the race of life, mounting the crags and cliffs of the cloud-capped hills until he sees the far horizons of the promised, the inevitable, but as yet the unachieved.

Sophocles and Phidias, Virgil, Anthemius of Tralles, the unknown builders of mediæval abbeys and cathedrals, the forgotten creators of the Nibelungenlied and the Arthurian legends; St. Gregory and his masters of music; St. Benedict Biscop and St. Dunstan with their craftsmen: Cimabue and Giotto and Leonardo; Dante and Shakespeare; Bach, Beethoven, Wagner, Browning — what are they and their fellows and peers but divinely constituted seers, clamant trumpets, prophets whose lips have been touched with the live coal of the altar of God; speaking now in the Pentecostal tongues of art, the which every man hears as his own language; hears and understands?

To every artist it is given so to voice something of that which is best and highest in man. To the sculptor no less than the poet, to the architect no less than the painter, to the dramatist and the maker of liturgies and ceremonial no less than the master of music. Each art has its own peculiar methods, the ordained instruments of its operation; but each is but a dialect of a normal language that reveals, in symbolical form and through the unsolvable mystery of beauty, all that men may achieve of the mystical knowledge of that Absolute Truth and Absolute Beauty that transcend material experience and intellectual expression, since they are of the essential being of God.

The artist is bound and controlled by the laws of his art, but doubly is he bound by his duty to society. If he is prohibited — as he is under penalty of æsthetic damnation — from denying beauty or contenting himself with expedients, or sacrificing any jot or tittle of the integrity of his art to fashion, or vulgarity, or the lust of evil things, still more is he bound to mankind by the law of *noblesse oblige*, and by the fear of God, to use his art only for the highest ends, to proclaim only the vision of perfection, to cleave only to the revelation of heavenly things. The architect who abandons himself to the creation of ugliness, however academic may be its *cachet;* the painter who "paints what he sees" or makes his art the ministry of lust; the sculptor who regards the form and sees nothing of the substance; the poet who glorifies the hideous shape of atheism, or the grossness of the accidents of life; the musician who exalts the morbid and the horrible; the maker of ceremonials who assembles depraved arts in a vain simulacrum of ancient and noble liturgies, — these are but traitors to man and God, and however competent their craft, they are enemies of the people, and to them should be meted the condemnation of their kind.

For many generations there has been too much of this, and the plea offered in extenuation, "The public demands it," is not a justification, but an intensification of criminality. It is vicious enough in journalism and politics, since it is the death-warrant of society, but it is ten times more evil in art, for the life-blood of art is the giving of something a little better than men consciously desire; the expression of the subconscious, which so often is the real man working deeply in the mysterious fastnesses of the soul. If the artist sells himself for bread, if he is driven by the harsh compulsion of poverty to sacrifice his art to Hydra, there should be pity for him on earth as there surely is mercy for him in heaven, but I know of no other justification for his sin. Even in the golden days when men could rename a road, calling it the Street of Rejoicing, because in a singing procession all the people of the quarter had carried through it to its altar in the parish church a new picture by a new painter, the art they acclaimed was good to them, not because it was the old and familiar art they knew, given them by the mechanical purveyors of Byzantine tradition, but because it was a newer and better thing, the picture in their hearts, not the picture in their minds. How much more, then, now that the popular instinct for beauty has become a craving for the hideous and the uncouth, how much more is it necessary that every artist, whatever the mode of his work, should lay down his life, if need be, in a last defence of the "something better," knowing his day, his year, his life to have been misspent if at the end of either one he could not say, "I have given better than was asked or expected of me."

Yet even in this, in the impulse that drives ever onward, that marks the artist as does his sense of beauty and his creative power, there is danger of the sharpest kind; the peril that lurks on the serpent tongue of the time-spirit, luring men into vain imaginings of "new art." It is a subtle and specious temptation; it comes with all the support of popular enthusiasms for breadth and liberality, personal emancipation and intellectual independence, humanism, and a certain temporal and racial self-consciousness. It is of the same ilk as that economic nervousness that devises pseudo-scientific panaceas for social and industrial ills; as that religious hysteria that fills the Saturday editions of the evening papers with astonishing advertisements of unearthly cults and wild philosophies: it asserts the need of new modes of expression for new manifestations of life, casting doubt and disfavour on old philosophies, old religions, old arts. Plato and Aristotle and St. Thomas Aquinas were well enough for their own time, and doubtless quite wonderful. The Catholic Faith, yes, Christianity itself, whatever its form, served excellently in an undeveloped stage of society and mental accomplishment. Gothic architecture was a good expression of its peculiar time. But we, now that the shackles of superstition have been shattered, now that the intellect is really emancipated and we have produced a civilization in comparison with which Hellas and the Roman Republic and the Christian Middle Ages were but as tentative beginnings, full of false steps and vagarious wanderings, *we* must create our own philosophy, our own religion, our own art.

And we try: whether Monism and Pragmatism, New Thought, Christian Science, and the "Church of the Higher Life," Matisse, Richard Strauss, and D'Annunzio achieve a degree of vital and enduring expression of essential things that gives them place above the philosophy, the religion, and the art of the past, is, I submit, a question susceptible of discussion. For my own part I am persuaded that they do nothing of the kind, but rather that what they produce is in no respect either new philosophy, new religion, or new art, but simply the troubled ferment of an epoch that, having lost its sense of proportion, fails to grasp either its own deficiencies or the notable advantages that are attributable to the times and the men and the works it now regards with a patronizing toleration.

And in holding this I do not lose sight of certain elements of value that exist in each one of the revolutionary and sometimes anarchical protests against a frozen tradition, the value of precisely this protest. As a matter of fact, we are bound hand and foot to a traditionalism that is Byzantine in its rigidity and mounts often to the level of an historic superstition. The nineteenth century, instead of being an era of emancipation, was the very age wherein were forged the most efficient shackles on true freedom of thought and action. Then were fixed in final form all the narrowing tendencies of modern life: the stolid formulæ that are making of parliamentary government a synonym for corruption and inefficiency; the pretensions of physical science that have turned religion out of house and home; the carnival of industrial activity that has threatened to revolutionize education into a wilderness of "institutes of commerce" and "vocational schools"; that has brought in a new and awful form of serfage and slavery and has almost overturned the ethical standards of society; the fanatical exaggeration of the value inherent in "free speech and a free press" that has built up an irresponsible and unprincipled engine that is fast becoming a menace to civilization; the literary standard of the "best seller," the dramatic standard of the "successful run," the academic and mechanical theories of art that metamorphose the gift of God into a series of hidebound formulæ that are taught as one teaches sanitary engineering or stenography.

In so far as the suffragettes and Mrs. Eddy and Matisse and Debussy and the prophets of "art nouveau" are a protest and a rebellion against the mordant superstitions of the nineteenth century, we may wish them well in their revolt, but when they assume to rebuild as well as to destroy, then we must arise to do them battle. The Renaissance broke a splendid path through a fast-thickening jungle, but once in the saddle, Machiavelli followed, and Alexander VI; the Reformation was a mighty destroyer of evil, but its substitutions were calamitous; the Revolution swept Europe clear of a pestilence that bred death and hell, but, conquering, it engendered a poison that still runs in the veins of society. The power that destroys can never under any circumstances rebuild; the conquerors in battle may never organize the victory, — a lesson the world seems never to learn even in its gray hairs. And so, for the artist, the very plausibility of the new revolutionists, the manifest righteousness of their crusade, wins a confidence in their constructive propaganda that is justified only in their campaign of destruction. It is true the Old Salon is simply an ever-renewed museum of mechanical toys that refuse to go, and when Matisse in decent scorn and disgust paints his protest in a kind of pictorial anarchy, when Cézanne thrusts gratuitous ugliness in the face and eyes of smug imbecility, we cheer them on, and are bound to come to their aid; but we are no more bound thereafter to their following than we should have been to that of Marat and Robespierre because we had taken part in the affair of the Tennis Court.

It would be folly to deny that our own era has innumerable elements of conspicuous novelty, many of them admirable and deeply to be desired, others no less loudly acclaimed, but essentially worthy only of condemnation. That the novel things are so radical in their nature, so Minerva-like in their spontaneous generation, that before them antiquity stands wondering and impotent, I venture to deny. Neither the hand, nor the mind, nor the soul of man has created or revealed during the last four centuries any single truth or aspect of truth that transcends the powers of expression of the philosophy, the religion, or the art of the past. New modes of expression, — yes, quite possibly; indeed, surely; but variety of expression does not involve a revolution in the fundamental law. The philosophy of St. Thomas did no violence to that of Aristotle; the religion of St. Bernard, or St. Francis, or St. Bonaventure was one with the religion of the Apostles; the art of the Middle Ages was based on the fundamental law of the art of Hellas; and yet how infinitely varied, how bright with the clear light of new dawns, how infused and palpitant with new blood, new visions, new revelations. The eternal laws that control the operations of the universe were effective before the nineteenth century, and they were perceived and acted upon before the invention of printing and the popularizing of experimental science and the emancipation of the intellect. New foundations there are none, new superstructures there must always be, endless in variety, better intrinsically, perhaps, than those we have known before, but if they are to be this, if they are to rank even in the same category with the wonders of the past, they must be wrought in obedience to the same laws that have held from the beginning of time.

Therefore, the artist who, fired by the outward diversity and the crescent vitality of the life that environs him and of which he is a part, steps beyond the bounds of possible variation in method and violates the eternal law of his art, ceases at that instant to be an artist and becomes a charlatan, and as such an enemy of the people.

All the art of every time is founded on some specific art of the past; without this there is no foundation save that of shifting sands. If it remains in bondage to this older art, if, like the Munich painting, the English architecture, the American sculpture of half a century ago, it wanders in the twilight of precedent or, in fear and trembling, chains itself to the rock of archæology, then again it ceases to be art — ceases? no; it has never even begun: it is only a dreary mocking of a shattered idol, a futile picture-puzzle to beguile a tedious day.

Between these perils on either hand, the temptation toward anarchical novelty, and the temptation toward archæological sterility, the artist falls often to the ground; to steer a safe course between Scylla and Charybdis, is hard, indeed, the more so in that the old landmarks, the old buoys and beacons have disappeared. If we only possessed at least the conviction that art is never wholly an end in itself, the problem would be simpler, but this knowledge we do not have. We are taught, indeed, the nobility of art, the varied and wonderful and hardly acquired methods of its accomplishment; but when our schools (which in several of the categories of art are vastly superior to any that have existed before) have accomplished their due task, life itself, either in its material or its spiritual aspect, does not step in to show the artist how to use his art toward the highest ends. In France, for example, architecture is taught more brilliantly and efficiently than anywhere else in the world; yet when a young man graduates from the École des Beaux Arts and seeks to put into practice the art he has acquired, what does he find for an environment, what are the powers and influences of society that are brought to bear on him for the development of his personality? Anarchy thinly veiled by socialistic nomenclature; religion a scorn and a laughing-stock; materialism supreme in nearly every department of life; education that is mechanical, and supposedly scientific, but with no faintest cognizance of the spiritual side of human nature; immorality rampant, and unchecked in its appalling increase. Is it any wonder that no French architect bred in the École since it was organized has brought into being any work whatever that belongs in the same class with that of the unlearned master-masons of the time four centuries ago when France was still a Christian nation?

Something of the same danger confronts us here in our own country, though nowhere in the world are the powers of evil marshalled so massively against righteousness as in unhappy France. So long as it is true, even in a measure, that the obvious and salient forces of society are leagued against the development of the spiritual and idealistic elements in man, so long will our schools of art fail of accomplishing their mission. They frame the law, but righteous life is itself the "enacting clause," and without this, legislation is inoperative.

There is a certain hedonistic view of life that breeds the doctrine that art is the product of luxury, culture, and ease. No more poisonous heresy was ever devised. The springs of art lie in right living and good citizenship and the fear of God. We may organize schools of architecture in every state; crowd the villas of Rome with ambitious young sculptors, and the Parisian ateliers with potential painters; we may patronize poets even to the point of giving them a living wage, and endow opera-houses and theatres in every village; our millionaires may shed their golden rain over a thirsty land, and public opinion may demand high art even if it has to get it with an axe — it is all but "vanity; feeding the wind and folly," as Sir Thomas has it, if beneath it all, the only enduring foundation, we have not a right attitude to ourselves, to our fellows, and to God.

But, men may say, perhaps, this is the affair of the Church and the school, of the teacher of ethics, the social reformer, the philosopher, and the priest. Not altogether, by any means. Art, rightly understood, rightly practised, is so wonderful a thing that it has many and varied aspects. Not only is it a revelation, it is an incentive: not only is it the flower, it is also the seed. Every art is at the same time vocative and dynamic: it voices the highest and the best; it subtly urges to emulation; it is perhaps the greatest civilizing influence in the world. Yet if it is a seed, it must fall neither amongst thorns, nor on stony ground, nor yet in a soil so rich that the weeds spring up and choke it. We deny this manifest truth of the civilizing potency of art for the very reason to which I alluded earlier, namely, that we estimate art by its highest reaches, and since these always came like the aftermath of harvest, when the fields of civilization had been reaped and the frosts of winter were at hand, the fertile seed shrivelled and perished and the fields remained barren and dead. When art was crescent, when it was the great outpouring through the chosen few of the spiritual experiences of a people, then it found its fertile soil, and the reward was an hundred fold.

If we believed, — which God forbid! — that we of this race and time and generation could offer nothing but an unfruitful soil, then were our labours vain; but while we know we come at the decadent end of one epoch of five centuries, it is gloriously true that we are at the very beginnings of yet another: the night is deep, but there is dawn on the uttermost hills. Before us lies the choice of fields for our sowing: if we turn to those that are exhausted by five centuries of reckless husbandry, to the fields of materialism and anarchy and infidelity, then our future is without hope; but if we go forward to the new lands of the new day, then there are no limits that may be placed on our service and our accomplishment.

In the very fact we deplore, that we have no immortal artists such as those of the great moments of the past, lies the cause of our greatest courage. Were this a time of art such as that which flung the radiant glamour of its matchless glory over the charnel-house of the Italy of the pagan Renaissance, then we might despair, for we should know that the issue was hopeless; but because of this, because we must lament our lack of art instead of exulting over its triumphant possession, we are full of courage, knowing that the tide has turned and that we are at the beginning of things, not at the lamentable end.

Before every artist of this day and generation open limitless and glittering possibilities. There is a new light on the hills, a new word on the wind, a new joy in the heart. France goes her way to the pit she has digged; England crumbles daily before our eyes; anarchy looms in the Latin countries of Europe; and we ourselves are for the moment staggered by persistent and mordant corruption in public, private, commercial, and industrial life; and yet we know these are the last things of an epoch only, not of a race; that they are episodes of a phase of growth and sequent decay, not the final revelation of the genius of a people. Already, though sometimes in baffling and devious ways, the new impulse is manifesting itself: again men turn to religion and to the everlasting things of the spirit, to law and order, to a new righteousness of life. For ourselves, the crash of crumbling superstitions and persistent error: for our children, the building of new mansions of righteousness and truth.

Therefore, there is for the artist a clear field: man is in revolt against materialism; thinking thoughts and dreaming dreams and seeing visions that cry aloud for utterance through that great agency of art that always in the past has answered the call and recorded in enduring monuments all that makes for nobility and righteousness in any race or time. Also, the ground is prepared for the sowing, and all that art can do toward furthering the process of a great regeneration may now be done with full effect. Rightly conceived and nobly executed, every work of art that is created in answer to the great new call of man may become an active agency in the momentous crusade. Church and college and school are, it is true, the prime educational and regenerating influences, but no one of these agencies, great as it is, can accomplish its completest destiny unless it recognizes the educational potency of art, and effects with it that alliance against which the powers of evil cannot prevail. Every church — nay, every building of whatever kind — that is infused with beauty and significance; every picture or statue that tells of eternal things through the same quality of sacramental beauty; every poem, every musical creation, every drama that exalts the sacred and hidden things of the soul over the flamboyant and futile phantasms of the world, becomes a living energy, an irresistible influence toward those very ends for the attainment of which the Church and the school exist.

Art may no longer remain "cribbed, cabined, and confined" in the private possession of those who can pay its price: as it is the language of the people, so must it become their free possession. Architecture has always been for all men, for none could hide its light — or darkness, perhaps — under a bushel; but all the other arts must come forth into the open, and in the Church, the school, the public buildings of city and state, offer themselves and their wide beneficence to all humanity. For centuries we have made great music, great pictures, great sculpture either an appanage of the rich, or the professionally venerating paraphernalia of an æsthetic curiosity shop, —

to be seen on payment of twenty-five cents on week days, free on Sundays and holidays. This is the nadir of civilization: better almost a generation that knew not even the name of art than one that so utterly misjudged it as so to misuse it. There may be some question as to whether free speech, a free press, and the electoral franchise are inalienable rights of the people; there is none as to the nature of art: either it is the divine heritage of all men, or it is nothing; if it is the ear-mark of a class, the privilege of a caste, it is no more than the monster of Frankenstein, a dead horror, moving and sentient, but without a soul.

This also is a part of the duty of the artist to the public, the giving back of the seven old lamps, heedlessly bartered for new. They cannot raise the potent genie of the fire and air, these new lamps, for all their rubbing. Give back the old lamps, and once more the

> "Djins and Afrits of the enchanted deep"

bow obedient, filling our hands with the overflowing treasures of the wonderland of the spirit and the soul.

To voice, to reveal, to prophesy; yes, and to fight manfully in the new crusade. There is besotted ignorance in the high places of the city and the state and the nation; there is an illustrated journalism that is working insidiously and overtime to break down not alone the new-found sense of beauty, but civilization itself; there is a popular drama — not the good old melodrama, that had some rough semblance of truth and beauty, but the new and horrible thing exploited by the racial enemies of Christianity — that finds its parallel only in the dark annals of toxicology; there is an insane rationalism in painting and sculpture that builds on the mad formula that the measure of art is its fidelity to the observed facts of nature; there is the on-rushing pestilence of bill-boards, the gross humbug of the art fakir, and a score of other depressing things of similar nature against which every civilized man must contend, but the artist more than all, for each is to him a personal insult, and he can see more clearly than others the menace they are, not only to him and to his art, but to the whole life of man that speaks through him.

There is war enough, God knows, and a field for good fighting. The artist who cares for his art, who knows what it means and why it is given him, knows also that his work is done not only in the studio, but on the field of action, in fierce fighting against the marshalled enemies of society and civilization, and for the bringing back to the people of their long-lost heritage.

And specifically there is one field where all these ends are furthered in one: I refer, of course, to art in its association with religion. A few years ago there was not this possibility: then religion reviled art and would none of it; then also it was the fashion to sneer at religious things and to consider them unworthy the attention of an emancipated intellect and beneath the dignity of a reputable artist. The results were not such as to encourage a persistence in these courses. Now it is no longer fashionable to sneer at religion, nor is it a mark of intelligence. Infidelity, agnosticism, indifference are now notes of an outgrown superstition, while the Church, roused from her long nightmare of iconoclasm, and worse, clamours for the aid of her old ally.

Above all things I pray that she may have it, both for her own sake and that of the artist, and that of society itself. If art is, indeed, as I have said, one of the really great agents of civilization, the Church is preëminently the place where its work may be made most effective. Beautiful buildings, pictures, and sculpture in schools and libraries, popular productions of the Greek and Elizabethan dramas, all are good and powerful influences toward education and regeneration; but the Church is more than all, for it has been, and is coming to be again, the great centre of spiritual energy. Each art is fine in itself, but a great and beautiful church, living with pictorial and sculptured decoration, where the sublime, appalling mystery of the Christian Faith is solemnized through the assembling of all the other arts — music, poetry, drama, and ceremonial — in one vast, organic work of art built up of every one of them raised to its highest level of possibility, and all fused in one consummate *opus Dei*, — this, the Catholic Mass in a Gothic church, is, in simple fact and in plain speech, the greatest artistic achievement, the most perfect proof of man's divine nature thus far recorded in the annals of humanity.

Here, above all other places, art performs its highest function, becomes most intimately the art of all the people, and gives to every artist his most perfect opportunity both for artistic expression and artistic service. In the new epoch that is even now at dawn, it will be, not in the palaces of captains of industry, or in any secular capacity whatever, that each and every art will find its opportunities both for creation and for service, but, as in the golden past, in churches and monastery chapels and cathedrals, themselves once more become, as also in that same past, the most essential, intimate, and important single thing in the life of every man.

Therefore, if the artist is to serve the public, he must become the proud and reverent ally of organized religion; first of all, winning back for himself the faith filched from him, and learning once more to speak the tongue God gave him and as it was taught him — whatever his art — by this same Church herself.

Is this too great a thing to ask? It has

happened over and over again in the past, and it must happen again: if not to-day, then to-morrow. Religion and the sacramental vision of Absolute Truth and Absolute Beauty are knit together by indissoluble bonds, and with them art is involved in a union that neither man nor devils may break asunder. The effort is made, and for a time it seems to be successful, but always and invariably the result is incalculable loss; to art, to religion, to the world. Religion wavers, yields to insidious heresies, breaks up into futile sects, fails to enforce its appeal to men; while art loses, first its highest ideals, then all ideals whatever; and finally follows after false leaders and silly theories, and so breaks down in ruin. This is the thing that has happened in the centuries that have followed the fall of Constantinople, and now once more begins the great recovery, the new epoch of restoration: already the ground gained amongst those of our own Northern blood and speech is enormous, but it must continue farther yet,—infinitely farther,—and the next step is inevitable. Alone, isolated, neither religion nor art can accomplish its destiny, which is to seize upon society and lift it to those heights of righteous achievement that have made and marked the eras of the past. Religion lacks its Pentecostal tongue; art lacks the Pentecostal flames of divine inspiration. The Church is conscious now of what this alliance will mean, for herself, for art, and for humanity: she is ready, with welcoming hands; and if the artist answers in kind, if he breaks the bonds of plausible materialism and rationalism, forsaking the exhausted fields of a squandered past for the fertile soil of a burgeoning future, then he will achieve that new life in his own spirit and in his art that is the guaranty of the fulfilment of the destiny that brought him into the world.

And here we find the revelation of the function of the artist in his relation to the world; in his choice between the two fields offered for his sowing. If he is false to the light within him, yielding his divine art for the pleasure of the votaries of pleasure; binding himself in servitude to the defiant corruption of a lost and ended cause; sitting in darkness and in the shadow of death; his reward is as theirs and he goes down to his appointed place with all other unfaithful servants. But if he chooses otherwise, making himself the mouthpiece of the new crusaders who march ever onward for the redemption of the holy places of the soul, answering the call of the best in man with the best that is in himself, revealing to humanity, through sacred beauty, the truth that shall make men free, consecrating himself to the showing, through whatever art where God has given him craft, "the light which lighteth every man that cometh into the world," then, for a time his reward may be poor in material measure, but in the end for him is reserved that crown of righteousness that is for them that are faithful and true, and that serve God through the serving of them that He made in His image and redeemed in the darkness and the thunderings of Calvary.

V

THE CRAFTSMAN AND THE ARCHITECT

V

THE CRAFTSMAN AND THE ARCHITECT[1]

IN its last Annual Report the Committee on Education of the American Institute of Architects laid particular emphasis on the relationship between the architect and the craftsman, pointed out the almost complete lack of good artificers in America and the shocking disparity between educational agencies in Europe and this country, and urged upon the architectural profession the paramount necessity of taking heed of the existing condition and the necessity of amending it without delay. The Report said in part:—

From time to time we have referred more or less casually to the fact that while we have the most copious and widespread architectural education to be found in any country, we have practically no agencies for the education of craftsmen. The result must be, and is, extremely injurious, if not fatal, to architecture itself. We may on

[1] Address at the convention of the American Federation of Arts in Washington.

paper create visions that rival those of Coleridge's Kubla Khan; we may on arising from a weary drawing board, our creative task accomplished, say with Justinian (and believe ourselves in the saying), "Solomon, I have surpassed thee," but when we see our drawings and our designs materialized in three dimensions we realize that, were we buried within their walls, the globe-trotting New Zealander, a century hence, looking for our personal monuments, would hardly say with Sir Christopher's eulogist, "Circumspice." In the good old days when an architectural monument was a plexus of all the arts, the architect was pretty much at the mercy of the craftsman, and he still is, with a difference; for then every bit of sculpture or painting or carving or metal-work and joinery, and glass and needle-work — when these latter came into play — enhanced the architecture, glorified it, and sometimes redeemed it as well; now either our carving is butchered, our sculpture and painting conceived on lines that deny their architectural setting, our metal-work turned out by the commercial ton, our stained-glass work defiant of every law of God, man, or architect, or it is all reduced to a dead level of technical plausibility, without an atom of feeling or artistry — and we are glad to take it this way, for the sake of escaping worse.

Every architect knows that the success or failure of his work depends largely on the craftsmen who carry it out and complete it with all its decorative features of form and colour, and yet in a nation of one hundred million people, with a dozen schools of architecture, practically nothing is done toward educating these same craftsmen, and we either secure the services of foreign-trained men, accept tenth-rate native work, or go without. Take a case in point; it is decided to build a metropolitan cathedral, with little regard to cost; plans are made (we will say satisfactorily), — what then? If it is to be a great and comprehensive work of art it needs (and exactly as much as it needs its architect) sculptors, painters, carvers in wood and stone, glassmakers, mosaicists, embroiderers, leather-workers. Are there enough schools in America to train all the craftsmen needed on this one monument, is there *one* school, and if so, where? One of the foolish arguments against Gothic is that it is quite dependent on artist craftsmen, and as we have none we must abandon the style; one of the foolish arguments in favour of Classical design is that anybody can learn to carve an acanthus, therefore we had better stick to what we know we can do. Neither argument is sound; if we have no artist-craftsmen, then it would be better for us to close up half the schools that are turning out architects and employ the funds for the training of the only men who can give life to the architects' designs.

Apart from the industrial arts in their relationship to architecture, their importance in this country, where art manufactures or products are so enormously in demand, is too obvious to need demonstration. Nearly all our expert labour in the artistic trades is imported from Europe. We pay large wages to foreign workmen, but refuse to educate our own people so that this financial benefit may accrue to them. In other words, our prosperity results in benefiting the alien, and we allow our own citizens to degenerate, furnishing no new employment for the rising generation, but fitting it only for those limited callings which are already overstocked, and in which it can command but a minimum wage.

The Report then summarized the educational activities of France, so far as the arts allied with architecture are concerned, and although even there some of the most important crafts are as yet unrecognized, it appeared that in three alone there were in Paris four hundred and twenty-five students with an annual budget of seventy-two thousand dollars. It then considered what is being done (or not done) in New York in the line of architectural modelling and painting, and after showing its extreme inadequacy, it continued: —

Now, if all this is true of architectural modelling and painting, it is at least equally true of the other arts, such as wood-carving, the making of stained glass, and metal-work of all kinds; obviously little is done educationally in any of those directions, and as a consequence when we want really good work we go abroad for it, or employ foreign-trained men who have taken up their residence in this country. Some time ago, a member of this Committee was asked to give a list of artist-craftsmen who were competent in design and execution, and who were willing to work with due regard to the architectural environment of their products; he reported that there were two Americans who were doing well as beginners in stained glass, but that it would be safer to go to England where the ancient tradition in design and workmanship still maintains in a measure; he named two good sculptors in wood, one a Bavarian, one a German; one admirable iron-worker, a German; one goldsmith, an Englishman; and two architectural sculptors, one a Welshman, the other American.

Of course, this is all wrong; there should be an hundred craftsmen in each category, if architectural dreams are to be properly materialized and embellished, and these should be our own people, not imported aliens, however competent they may be.

It should be understood that we are not referring to the sculptor and painter as architectural allies; we have great men in both categories, and their relationship to the profession was considered by the Committee on Allied Arts of last year; we are speaking of the craftsmen whose work enters more intimately into the ordinary architectural practice, and so speaking we do not hesitate to say that the present state of things is barbarous, uneconomical, and in the last degree discreditable to the architectural profession.

"Barbarous, uneconomical, and discreditable," these words are none too strong to apply to a condition of things which has endured for long, and even now fails to arouse indignation, or even a measure of recognition. I could make a strong case against the present system, or lack of system, on economic grounds alone, showing how unpatriotic, unbusinesslike, and unpractical it is for America to deny to its own citizens a field of work that is remunerative and that must be filled, so putting a premium on the alien workman who has been able to acquire his dominant proficiency in his native and more generous land; a strong case also against the labour unions that disparage the apprentice system, and discourage the spirit of emulation that results in individual advancement and consequently increased returns to the specially able men; a strong case, finally, against a system that simply means that for many products of the artist-craftsman the owner or architect must perforce go across the ocean, paying his money not even into the hands of foreign-born American citizens, but to foreign residents, and then paying his further tax as well to the National Government for the protection of American producers, who, so far as the essential element in the product is concerned, — quality, — simply do not exist.

It would be interesting to go into the matter in detail and show the barbarism and the dull ignorance of the present condition, but, for the moment, I must waive this and confine myself to the matter that more closely affects the owner and the architect, and that is the heavy handicap that is placed on every one, lay or professional, who tries to create some work of art that shall be not only acceptable in idea, but even tolerable in its working-out.

Now, why is it that in spite of the most complete and effective architectural education the world has ever known, wealth that could buy the labour that built the pyramids, that made

Chartres Cathedral almost a revelation of Divinity, and fretted the lacey fabric of the Taj Mahal, and as many practising architects in the directory of a great city as all Europe numbered during the whole epoch of mediævalism, — how is it that with these notable advantages we cannot succeed in building one structure to match a minor Greek temple, a second-class mediæval monastery, or a provincial Buddhist shrine of twelfth-century Japan? There are, I think, three reasons; the first two do not concern us at this moment, the third very much does. I name the two first, for nobody can stop me, — an abandonment of definite and concrete and inspiring religious conviction, and our disregard of the sound principles of law and order and obedience, — and having named them, we shall hear no more of them at this time. The third is precisely that which is the subject of this paper, the disappearance of the individual, independent, and self-respecting craftsman, and by this third loss, we are left helpless and hopeless, indeed; for as the Renaissance demonstrates, the real craftsman can do much, as he did do much, to make amends for the loss of greater things, and, so long as he endures, as through the Renaissance he *did* endure, can raise an inferior architecture to a level of credit that in itself it could not claim, while giving to an equally inferior civilization a glamour of glory that rightly could not proceed from its own inherent nature.

We may sit spellbound before the august majesty of the École des Beaux Arts, and to it, by grace of a generous French Government, we may send our boys by hundreds; we may found, equip, and endow schools of architecture in every college in America; we may rear architectural museums in every state, establish architectural lectureships that will subject the railways to an unfair test of their carrying capacity, and crowd the transatlantic steamships with eager holders of travelling studentships, — it will be of little avail if we cannot entrust our dreams and our working drawings to genuine craftsmen for the carrying-out, but instead find ourselves compelled to hand them over to the tender mercies of general contractors, "Ecclesiastical Art Decorators and

Furnishers," and department stores where the watchwords are "efficiency," division of labour, and "You give us sketches. We do the rest."

By itself architecture is nothing; allied with the structural crafts and the artist crafts, it is everything, — the greatest art in the world; for it is a plexus of all the arts; it assembles them in a great synthesis that is vaster than any art by itself alone, that gathers them together in the perfect service of God and man.

Without the craftsman an architectural design is worth little more than the paper on which it is drawn; it is an ephemera, a simulacrum of glory. From a distance, or at first sight, it may have majesty of form, power of composition, impressiveness of silhouette, and richness of light and shade, but close at hand, it is a dead thing, without a vivifying soul, and it neither reveals the heart of a people, nor eats itself into their affections so that for them or their successors it becomes what to us to-day are the monuments of Greece and Byzantium and the Catholic Middle Ages. With the artist-craftsman, working independently but in close alliance, we may have again a San Marco, a Chartres, or a Seville — if, as well, our faith and our works are as those of them that built those wonders and enriched them with their splendour of decoration.

We exercise ourselves over the manifold questions of the faculties and the curriculums of the architectural schools in which we take such justifiable pride; we found one scholarship after another, and incessantly multiply our architectural lectureships and exhibitions; we even animatedly discuss the possibility of that plainly desirable thing, — a post-graduate school of architecture in Washington; and all the while we see with equanimity our designs butchered or frozen to death, our ornaments and furnishings provided by others than our own people, and usually in a perfectly commercial and mechanical manner at that; and finally we are content that our buildings should become, not the rich and opulent showing-forth of a great civilization through innumerable allied arts, but, instead, academic essays in theoretical design expressing nothing but the genius — or otherwise — of the architect, even to the machine-chiselled carving, the stencilled colour and the cast-plaster ornaments, all from his own full-size designs worked out by his own draughtsmen.

Think how the carved capitals of Lincoln, the statues of Wells and of Rheims, the inlay of Monreale, the mosaics of Ravenna and of the Trastevere, the glass of Bourges and of Chartres, the frescoes of Assisi, the grilles and "retables" of Seville and of Salamanca and of Mexico, the joinery of Henry the Seventh's Chapel and of Toledo, the metal-work of Nuremberg — consider how all these were made, and why and when, and then exult over our triumphant civilization, or marvel that all the wealth and all the architects and artists of the world could not rival to-day or equal the Capella Palatina in Palermo, which was merely the private chapel of a second-rate prince, in a frontier land in the dusk of the Dark Ages.

Of course, the basic reason for this deplorable condition of things is economic; it finds its root in the fantastic substitution, during and after the Renaissance, in place of a communism that developed true personality, of an individualism that destroyed personality. As the splendid liberty of mediæval society has hardened into a mechanical and irresponsible despotism that preserves only the empty name of liberty, so the triumphant individuality of the Renaissance has hardened into an economic system that, through mechanics, capitalism, the wage system, and division of labour, has become a very sordid kind of slavery. To effect a vital, comprehensive, and enduring reform, we should have to strike deep, and elsewhere than in the domain of art; but something can be done in a tentative and partial sort of way, pending the coming of that inevitable revolt and revolution that will "make all things new," for in minor ways, both the public that builds and the architect that serves this public are to blame. As a result of the economic revolution of the past three centuries, the architect has fallen into the habit of thinking that architecture is all there is to architecture; that planes and contours and spacings of light and shade make up his art; that ornament and furnishings are adventitious, anyway; and that, in any case, whatever is to be done by way of embellishment can best be done by highly specialized draughtsmen, under his own direction, with adequate photographs and reliable books and plenty of brown paper, charcoal, and tube colours, — together with a system of supervising the human and mechanical engines that turn these two-dimension creations into three dimensions during an eight-hour day and subject to the regulations of the labour unions.

Well, perhaps it can — as conditions now are; but if so we had better change the conditions. Just so long as the architect makes a blanket contract with a general contractor, or turns over his carving and sculpture to a well-capitalized corporation of stone-masons, or abandons his colour embellishment to some plausible organization of "decorators," or his church or palace to an august Fifth Avenue establishment, or his windows and his metal-work to an admirably advertised syndicate of artists with sufficient capital behind it to insure easy and pleasant conditions for all concerned, — just so long will he produce nothing that will outlast his lifetime, or give joy to any one concerned.

For it is not a case of no alternative; there are real craftsmen living to-day, and in this country, and turning out exquisite work after the ancient fashion, though Heaven knows why it should be so. I know three makers of tiles and other products of burnt clay and glazes, who are consummate artists (one of them is a woman), and who are to be dealt with only as individuals, and who, if they are treated as allies, not as commercial purveyors of trade goods, can glorify any building with which they come in contact; I know two workers in forged and wrought iron who are blood brothers of Adam Kraft; three goldsmiths who would gladden the heart of Cellini; a woodcarver who is Peter Vischer restored to life; two sculptors who are really architectural sculptors as were the men who immortalized Chartres and Wells; a stone cutter whose craft matches that of the masons of Venice and Rouen; a maker of stained glass who needs only opportunity to restore some measure of the wonder of this lost art; a maker of ecclesiastical vestments whose needlework is that of the fifteenth century; a scribe who can do real missals and other illumination as these once were done long ago. And not one of them has really enough to keep him busy or return him more than a living wage, while by default thousands of dollars worth of work they could do consummately goes weekly to factories and similar places where it becomes simply so much plausible sham.

Now, it is the manifest duty of the architect to search out these individual craftsmen and to bring them into alliance with himself. You will note that I speak of an "alliance," for this is almost the crux of the whole matter; whoever the craftsman is he must work with and not for the architect, although the latter must exercise a general oversight over everything, and form in a sense the court of last resort. Really an architect is, or should be, more a coördinator than a general designer; he should be a kind of universal solvent, by means of which architectural designers, workmen, artificers, craftsmen, and artists should come together, and, while preserving their own personality, merge their identity in a great artistic whole, somewhat as the instruments of a great orchestra are assembled to the perfect rendering of a symphony by the master and conductor.

This free field for the exercise of personality was always accorded the artist and the craftsman during that greatest and most successful of building epochs, the Middle Ages, and that it is now denied is due quite as much to the grasping nature of the architect as it is to the progressive degeneracy of the craftsman. The two elements are interrelated; as the craftsman decayed, the architect more and more took into his own hands the work he could not get well done elsewhere, and as he did so he discouraged and destroyed the craftsman already on the downward path.

Now, there is no reason why the architect should have to design his carving and tiles and glass and metal-work and joinery and colour decoration, except that no one else can do it, and when he does, by default, the result is only a poor and unenduring expedient. Now that true craftsmen are beginning to emerge from the welter of commercialism, it is, as I have said, the manifest duty of the architect to search them out and give them not only the preference, but the utmost measure of liberty of action of which they are worthy. What we are looking for, and what was always obtained in the epochs of high civilization, is not merely technical proficiency, but such proficiency united to creative capacity. There is no true craftsman who is not the personal designer of what he fashions, and it is the negation of this principle that vitiates so much of the work produced through the so-called "arts and crafts" societies of the present day. For my own part, I have lost much of my confidence in a movement that once seemed to promise so much, just because I have found there the same old vicious system; one man making the design, the other carrying it out. This is fatal, and I believe that the arts and crafts movement is doomed to immediate failure unless it prohibits absolutely the showing or selling or approval of any work that is not fashioned by the man who designed it, or is not designed by the man who fashioned it.

It is better to accept work that is in a measure defective, if it is so created, than a more perfect and plausible product that involves division of labour. I have in mind a certain woodcarver who cuts his statues directly from baulks of oak, without the intervention of either sketch or model, and though I am not always wholly in sympathy with what he does, though sometimes there is a naïveté in what he does that would scandalize a trained sculptor or a purist architect, I would not change this for a moment; for if I did, it would mean the achievement of efficiency and regularity at the expense of a better thing, and that is personality.

Of course, there are at present very few men who can be trusted implicitly, but there are many who have, and show, promise of possible development, and such men should be encouraged and given the widest possible latitude. They will repay this confidence tenfold, and considerate guidance linked with confidence and opportunity will give surprising results. I should like to suggest, therefore, that a kind of "White List" be compiled and published, and added to from time to time, of those craftsmen who have shown the ability and the promise; that it be given the widest publicity amongst architects, and that they should consider themselves bound in honour to go to these men, and work with them, rather than over them, in preference to the more august and widely heralded concerns that commend themselves rather by their financial than their artistic capital.

In the end, and that we may finally get back to the old and ideal state of things, we shall have to restore the ancient guild idea, and as well the workshops assembled around some great architectural undertaking. If a cathedral is to be built, or a university, or a public library, with the turning of the first sod should go the raising of temporary workshops, and the assembling of the varied workers that will be brought into play for the embellishing of the fabric. Think what a future cathedral close might be; in the midst, the slowly rising walls, and all around, busy workshops; here a group of stone-carvers under a competent foreman (but minus special designers and modellers), surrounded by casts and photographs and drawings of the carving of Chartres and Rheims and Venice and Wells and Lincoln; here glass-workers with their models from Bourges and Chartres and York, slowly fashioning (each man his own window) the jewelled filling for the tracerized apertures of the temple; here joiners and woodworkers with the same kind of surroundings, and workers in wrought and forged iron, and in gold and silver; tilemakers, with their Dutch and Persian and Spanish models; and so on, until all the varied list is filled. Each group would form its own independent guild, self-governing, self-controlled; all united then in a general guild which would have a broad supervision of all that was done, and provide models, books, teachers, while the architect himself would go daily through all the works, suggesting here, correcting there, inspiring everywhere. And with the primary craft activity would go also certain social elements, that would bind the several guilds together and give them coördination; educational elements, religious elements, and those features of assurance against loss through sickness and of participation in a division of profits, that were fundamental in the guilds of the Middle Ages. Can there be any doubt as to the result?

If such a thing as that could come into being in connection with one great contemporary building, it would mean that the problem was solved, and that for the future there would be enough real craftsmen and a better art, and a higher civilization.

You will say this is a dream impossible of achievement; that no owner would for a moment think of financing such a venture; that enough workmen could not be found to man any one of the workshops even if an adequate foreman could be obtained; that the idea of team work has so utterly died out of a hyper-individualized generation that a communal spirit could not be built up; and that such a scheme, if started, would immediately disintegrate through jealousy, suspicion, and avarice; and finally that the labour unions would refuse to permit anything of the kind and would destroy it, if initiated, by the simple method of calling a strike amongst the labourers on the works but outside the guilds.

I admit the force only of the last claim, and even here I think it is exaggerated. I cannot believe that organized labour could be so shortsighted as to fail to see that such a scheme was quite in harmony with the high ideals they openly avow; and if they were, I am sure the time is close at hand when the growing force of public opinion will suppress with a heavy hand the corruptions of unionism which are so unrepresentative of, and injurious to, its better principles.

However this may be, the thing must come and will come, for we cannot much longer submit to a condition so unwholesome and so deplorable in its results, or even to a type of civilization that makes this condition inevitable. If individualism or commercialism or division of labour or the trade unions stand in the way, they will be swept out of existence, going down in defeat before the resolution that will surely in its progress bring back again many of the old conditions that marked, as they will ever mark, estates of high civilization. In the mean time, we can — and I close as I began — do much toward the amelioration of no longer endurable conditions, much even toward the bringing-in of the great and fundamental reforms. I doubt if the state can do this, for its achievements in the line of popular education are not such as to enlist confidence; it is too blackly tarred with the same stick of secularism, mechanism, and the division of labour. I doubt if the schools and colleges can do it, or would do it. But the architect can, and the owner, for both can make the demand and foster and further the supply. It is to them, therefore, that we must turn in our emergency; to the owner, in the hope that he will demand real craftsmanship and accept no commercial or syndicated substitute; to the architect, in the confidence that he will search out the individual craftsman, give him the preference, and accord him the greatest measure of liberty of which he is worthy — and even a little more. And in these hopes we shall not be disappointed, for once the condition is recognized there is no alternative, — action, immediate, comprehensive, and persistent, becomes a matter of honour.

VI

AMERICAN UNIVERSITY ARCHITECTURE

VI

AMERICAN UNIVERSITY ARCHITECTURE[1]

IT would be impossible for me to express in any adequate fashion my deep appreciation of the honour you do me in asking me to supplement, in some small degree, the penetrating and comprehensive paper Mr. Warren already has read before you, with a consideration and a showing of that other collegiate architecture over-seas which, as he so justly says, is in its impulse and its achievement a natural continuation of British tradition. We have in America, as you in your colonies, the residential college — the early, the perfect, the indestructible type — elsewhere abandoned, and with great loss in respect to those results in character-building (and therefore national civilization) for which no intensive scholarship can ever make amends. The foundations of sane and sound and wholesome society are neither

[1] Read before the Royal Institute of British Architects, London, 1912.

industrial supremacy, nor world-wide trade, nor hoarded wealth; they are personal honour, clean living, fearlessness in action, self-reliance, generosity of impulse, good-fellowship, obedience to law, reverence, and the fear of God,—all those elements which are implied in the word "character," which is the end of education and which is the proudest product of the old English residential college, and the old English educational idea that brought it into being, maintained it for centuries, and holds it now a bulwark against the tides of anarchy and materialism that threaten the very endurance of civilization itself.

From time to time we have yielded more or less to novel impulses, coquetting with that questionable lady sometimes known as the "Spirit of the Age," accepting even her insidious doctrine that, after all, the object of education is not the building of character, but the breeding of intensive specialists, or the turning of a boy at the earliest possible moment into a wage-earning animal. We still hold to the damnable opinion that education may be divorced from religion, and ethics inculcated apart from a dogmatic religious faith, and having sown the wind of an insane secularism, we are reaping the whirlwind of civic corruption and industrial anarchy. I do not mean to say that we were alone in our error: you yourselves know that across narrower seas than the Atlantic the same is true, and in greater degree, while even here, in these narrow islands that so often have been the last refuge and stronghold of Christian civilization, I have heard strange rumours of those who would sacrifice Latin and Greek and the humanities to applied science and vocational training; who would drive the very name of religion from the schools; who would, in the ringing words of an eminent French statesman, "put out the lights in heaven," and, to quote Karl Marx, "destroy the idea of God which is the keystone of a perverted civilization." We have, I think, rather got beyond taking this sort of thing seriously, and I doubt if you ever will do so even for a moment; for when we stop doing things long enough to think, we all realize that, as the Dean of St. Paul's has recently said, "The real test of progress is the kind of people that a country turns out," and the product of secularized and intensive education is not of a quality that develops in sane and healthy minds a sense either of covetousness or emulation.

So, in spite of our backing and filling, we are, I think, in America, well beyond the turn of the tide. I myself have seen it at its flood, and I have seen the ebb begin. It is not so long ago that our ideal seemed to be a kind of so-called education that might be labelled "made in Germany": we prescribed nothing, and accepted anything a freshman in his wisdom might elect; we joined schools of dental surgery and "business science" (whatever that may be) and journalism and farriery to our august universities; we ignored Greek and smiled at Latin; we tried to teach theology on an undogmatic basis (an idea not without humour), and we cut out religious worship altogether. It was all evanescent, however; now the "free electives" are passing, even at Harvard where they began and ran full riot; at Princeton the preceptorial system has been restored, and is coming elsewhere; there, also, a great college chapel is contemplated, while at the University of Chicago one is about to be built at a cost of some three hundred thousand pounds. Everywhere residential quads are coming into existence: one ancient college — Amherst — is considering abandoning all its scientific schools and falling back on the sound old classical basis, while lately our own American Institute of Architects has endorsed the principle that our schools of architecture should grant degrees only to those reasonably proficient in Latin.

And so we return step by step to the old ideals and sound methods of English colleges; return to the mother that bore us, just as we return year after year to our old home for refreshment and inspiration; return, even in a wider sense, to those eternally battered but eternally enduring principles in life and thought and aspiration which make up the great Anglo-Saxon heritage of which we proudly claim to be joint heirs with yourselves. And in this return we find ourselves recurring once more to the very forms of the architecture — or rather, we hope, to its underlying spirit — through which this great tradition has manifested itself. In our earliest days we followed, as closely as we could, the work going on at home; then we yielded to our new nationality and wandered off after strange gods, — some of them very strange, indeed, — expressing our experiments in experimental styles until the last shadow of a memory of England seemed wholly gone; and then, as the last flicker died, behold a new restoration! for with the reaction toward a broader culture comes the return to the architecture of Eton and Winchester, Oxford and Cambridge, that so fully expressed that very culture itself.

Consider for a moment and you will see that no other course was possible: not because the fifteenth and sixteenth and early seventeenth century collegiate architecture of England is the most perfect style ever devised by man to this particular end. It is this, of course, but the real reason for our return lies deeper, and it is simply that it is the only style that absolutely expresses our new-old, crescent ideals of an education that makes for culture and makes for character. I myself have been coming back to Oxford and Cambridge year after year now for a full generation, others for even longer terms; and every year I send, from my own and from other offices, boys and young men, to the same shrines of causes, not lost, but gone before, who are all of them beginning the same cycle of periodicity that has marked the lives of their elders; and to all of us, young and old, these gray and wonderful cities mean, not great art alone, but, even more, the greater impulse that incarnated itself in such personalities as Duns Scotus and Henry V; Sir Philip Sidney and Sir Walter Raleigh; Grocyn, Linacre, and Erasmus; Laud, and Strafford and Falkland; Hampden and Cromwell, the Duke of Wellington, John Keble, and Cardinal Newman. For one thing we know, at least, and that is that architecture, together with all art, is no matter of fashion or predilection, no vain but desirable amenity of life, but rather an unerring though perishable record of civilization, more exact than written history, and the only perfect showing of the civilization of a time. By its fruitage of art we know the tree of life, and further we know that this fruit is not seedless, but the guaranty of life to such ages as use it rightly. We love it for what it is in itself; more for what it reveals to us of a great past; most of all, for what it promises our future. Art has dynamic potency; it records, indeed, but it is evocative also; and we who would have Sidneys and Straffords and Newmans to redeem and defend and ennoble our civilization use the architecture that is their voicing that it may re-create their spirit in a later age and in a distant but not alien land.

So much, then, by way of the introduction you did not bring me over-seas to say; and now let us turn to the work itself of which you expect me to speak.

And first of all let me show you from Harvard one or two examples of what we did for a beginning. It was n't very much, I suppose, but we care for it extremely, just because it spells our own brief antiquity, while it was honest and sincere, and not without a certain pathetic element of far-away longing for an old but not forgotten home. English it was, of course, so far as we could make it, for we were all English, — or rather British, — in bone and blood and tradition, down to half a century ago. The old artistic impulse that had remained with man from the beginning was slowly dying, for the first time in recorded history; it had been losing vitality ever since the Renaissance and Reformation, but it was still instinctive, and so remained until that Revolution, which included so much more than the French Terror, came to give it its quietus. This day — or night — was still far off, and in the seventeenth and eighteenth centuries there was still exquisite delicacy and refinement and wealth of invention. I wish I could show you some proofs of this in the shape of domestic and ecclesiastical work from Massachusetts Bay Colony, and Virginia and Maryland and the Carolinas, for it is true that little of this appears in our collegiate work. Here funds were scant and dearly obtained, while the planters of the South and the great merchants of the North were more lavish in their outlay; as it is, our early college buildings make their appeal through their fine proportions and their frank simplicity.

Of course practically all the seventeenth-century work, and nine-tenths of that of the eighteenth is gone, including much of the best, and we must re-create our vision of the past from shreds and patches; but fortunately at Harvard there remains a notable group that has yielded neither to vandalism nor conflagration. As you will see from the plan of the old "Yard," the typical English quadrangular arrangement was abandoned for a grouping of isolated buildings, at first more or less formal, then developing into final chaos as other men with other minds came on the scene and placed their buildings, and designed them also, at their own sweet will. As for the material, it was almost invariably brick, at first imported from the old country, for the visible stone supply in New England was intractible granite, and even where a kinder material was available, there was in the beginning little skill in cutting, and later little money to pay for the labour involved. With few exceptions the trimmings of doors and windows and cornices were of delicately moulded wood painted white, the Vignolan laws as to proportion being intelligently modified to fit the new material, while the roofs were covered with split shingles.

The first evidence of decadence appears, I think, in the advent of that more pompous style Jefferson did so much to advance.

Hitherto what had been done was done simply and unaffectedly; now came the conscious desire for architecture, which is a dangerous ambition at best. At the University of Virginia we have the original setting out, almost intact, and if we deplore the unnecessarily unreasonable classical porticoes, with columns, entablatures, and pediments complete, — and all built of deal boards framed up in the semblance of a newly discovered paganism, — we must admit the great dignity of the plan and the singular charm of the ensemble.

This "Jeffersonian" style rapidly took the place of the old Georgian, but its day was brief; and somewhere between 1820 and 1830 occurred that ominous point when the last flickering tradition of good taste and the last weak impulse of instinctive art vanished, and the new era began wherein the desires and predilections of society as a whole were no longer for good things and beautiful things, but explicitly and even clamorously for bad things and ugly things, while the uncertain offices of the architect were the only agencies that from time to time redeemed the general chaos.

Fortunately, there was little collegiate building with us during this dismal second quarter of the nineteenth century, or rather, and also fortunately, little of it has survived; and when first the architect appears on the scene as the mentor rather than the exemplar of public opinion, it is in novel guise, nothing less, indeed, than as the protagonist of Gothic. He was not *very* Gothic, I must admit, and in the beginning he contented himself with a few apologetic and quite casual buttresses, pointed arches over his door and window openings, an octagonal turret or two, and of course battlements, usually of two-inch deal neatly painted, and sometimes sprinkled with sand as a concession to appearances. What took place in domestic and ecclesiastical architecture, I dare not even reveal to you, but the college work was a shade less horrific; for sometimes, as at West Point, it was of stone, and good stone work will cover a multitude of sins — as it still does in our own day and generation, I believe.

Perhaps it is hardly fair to attribute this first "Gothic" to architects; really it was the work of the ambitious builder who, after crystallizing under the immortal Batty Langley's handbooks on classical architecture, suddenly expanded with almost explosive force beneath the influence of that amazing work of the same gifted author wherein he reduces Gothic also to a system of "orders" and demonstrates how by a few simple rules one can easily learn to produce "genteel and appropriate Structures in the Gothic Taste." But the Oxford Movement and Pugin's Gothic Revival soon passed beyond the admirable Batty Langley, and the influence of Pugin himself entered America, largely through a really great architect, Upjohn. I think he did no collegiate work, but John Ruskin produced those that did, and from the close of our War between the States down to about 1880, the new Gothic that expressed his really enormous influence might be said to have run riot through our colleges. There were those like Renwick and Congdon, and Mr. Haight (who is still living), that held conscientiously to the grave and archæological type established by the Pugins; there were others who tried to incorporate Ruskinian doctrines in more personal, original, and mobile work, as Blomfield and Butterfield were doing here in England. The results were at least lacking in monotony, but few of them achieved the simplicity and the dignity of Mr. Haight's work, while many of them reached a point of violence and anarchy hardly to be matched in history.

It was all a "false dawn," however, and ceased almost in a moment (though for a brief period only, as we shall see) when that great genius and greater personality, Richardson, flashed like an unpredicted comet across the sky. The later seventies were desperate, no less; and the group of conscientious men could not withstand the flood of falsity and bad taste and artificiality that involved the whole art of architecture. Richardson alone turned the tide, brushed away the whole card-house of artifice, and deliberately forced a new and alien style on a bewildered people. He did great work, some of it immortal work, in his powerful mode; but he died before his mission was accomplished, and though he killed the "French roof style" and the futile Gothic, and all the other absurdities, he left behind no one of his own calibre to carry on the crusade, but instead a multitude of imitators who, though at first doing fine work under the memory and inspiration of their master, gradually turned away into other fields, leaving the Romanesque propaganda to the most inadequate exponents imaginable. For a decade we wallowed in lilliputian cyclopeanism, and then, to change the simile, the summer storm swept west and south, and over the desolation it had left loomed, almost simultaneously, three new tendencies, Colonial, Perpendicular Gothic, and "Beaux Arts." Three less well-assorted bedfellows it would be hard to find, but with a magnanimity rare in history these three rivals more or less succeeded in establishing a *modus vivendi*, Colonial taking over part of the new, and again triply divided, Gaul, in the shape of domestic work; Gothic annexing, so far as it could, all collegiate, scholastic, and ecclesiastical building; while to the Beaux Arts propaganda fell all it could get of the rest — particularly Carnegie libraries, town houses, and banks. As a matter of fact, this partitioning of architectural activity was not the result of amity, nor was it in the least definitive: the Colonial style claimed the patronage of our nonconformist brethren (with show of reason and propriety), Gothic tried vainly to break into the library fold, while the Beaux Arts architects made unavailing eyes at the Church, and, indeed, claimed everything in sight. Their pretensions did not go without questioning, however, for in the mean time the old and most classical Classic was re-born (it had never wholly died), and at the hands of that great man, Charles McKim, it suddenly achieved a height of serene nobility where it could and did challenge the claims of its rivals. And there were other claimants for the architectural crown now so completely "in commission": there was the Spanish pretender with its doubtful offspring, the quaintly denominated "Mission style"; there was the secessionist Americanism of the inspired but unguarded Mr. Sullivan; there was a kind of neo-Byzantinism; there was a hidden but persistent Japanese propaganda. In fact I was wrong when I said that the architectural Gaul was divided into three parts: it is not such a triple partition that confronts us now, it is an omnivorous eclecticism that bears some of the ear-marks of anarchy. To use one of our own phrases, "everything goes," and much of it goes exceedingly well, amazingly so, in fact; but the result is somewhat lacking in the qualities of unity and lucidity.

Fortunately, we have to do with few of the varied schools, for though all of them have footholds in the several colleges, only two have established their claims, Georgian and Gothic, and at the present time the latter has the call and has produced the most notable results: it may almost be said that, except where lack of funds or climatic conditions argue against Gothic, this has the field absolutely to itself. The ascetic and fastidious classicism of McKim created Columbia University and occurs sporadically elsewhere; the Boulevardesque of the Beaux Arts men appears in a single building at Yale, and in the slow-growing University of California and the Naval College at Annapolis; Spanish elements go to the making of Leland Stanford; and in Texas my own firm is doing "a deed without a name" that you must judge for yourselves and justify if you can and as we do ourselves. Elsewhere it is, as I said, Georgian or Gothic, and to the college trustee it is now the question, "under which King, Bezonian." Harvard, after swinging the circle of every possible architectural dogma and heresy, seems to have settled down, as she should, to Georgian, as has Williams, and so many of the smaller and poorer preparatory schools and colleges, particularly in the South; but Yale, West Point, Pennsylvania, New York, Princeton, Bryn Mawr, Washington University, St. Louis, and Chicago, together with all the larger preparatory and Church schools, and the newer Roman Catholic institutions, are uncompromisingly Gothic of the type made immortal in England.

Before showing you the nature of this work, it may be well to examine a typical American university, in its setting-out, in its component parts, and in its organization. I will choose for this purpose Princeton, of which I am a member by adoption and where I have the honor to act as supervising architect. The title itself will indicate at once one of the many points of divergence between the English and American systems, for I fancy there is no university in the United Kingdom where one man is given almost complete authority over all matters of the choice of architects, supervision of their work both in design and execution, acceptance or rejection of gifts and their placing if accepted, the development of roads and paths, and the planting of trees and shrubs. Until recently such an office was unknown in America, but since Princeton took the lead, some five or six years ago, others have followed rapidly and the practice has now become an established custom.

It was time, too, that something should be done: as I have already indicated, our colleges were like Topsy — they "just growed" — without rhyme or reason, subject to the most vacillating fashion and the quaint whims of emancipated individualism, while the results were generally shocking. In the plan of Princeton you will easily see how lawless had been the growth, and conditions were even worse at Harvard and Yale. You will note at once from the wide spacing and the lack of coördination another point of difference: with us almost every college has begun in open country, as an original foundation. We have nothing like Oxford and Cambridge, partly because of this fact, and partly because each college is with us a unit; we have no gathering up of many and independent foundations, loosely knit together for administrative purposes: we have instead self-contained units, sometimes of enormous size, and each new benefactor founds, not a new college, but a dormitory, a library, a school of law or medicine or forestry or — journalism. Personally, I think this plan must be abandoned, and a breaking-up into more manageable units take place. It seems to me demonstrable that in schools that have from four to six thousand students half the character-building qualities of education are lost, and that the personal element must be regained by breaking up these unwieldy masses into working units of not more than two hundred men each, at least for living and social purposes. This was attempted two years ago at Princeton, but the time was not ripe and the reform failed; still the leaven is working at Harvard and Cornell and elsewhere, and is, I think, within measurable distance of accomplishment.

In the new plan of Princeton, which shows the university as it now is, and indicates its future lines of development, you will see at once how strong the tendency is toward the standard type: here the dormitories are assuming quadrangular form, and in time may become full residential colleges, each with its common room and great hall and, when times have still further changed, perhaps its chapel. In the beginning our dormitories were simply barracks, with living rooms opening off long halls, with startling results so far as order and discipline were concerned. Now the "entry" type is almost universal, the type that holds in England, while the old sequence of regular cells serving both as study and bedroom for one or even two men, with a common *necessarium* two or three hundred yards away, has given place to the standard type of suites consisting of a study and two bedrooms for two undergraduates, and a study and bedroom for each graduate student. In the former case each stairway is separated from the next by a party wall, unbroken except in the basement to which all staircases descend, and here a general corridor gives access to groups of baths and toilets, and to the box-rooms, and to the other staircases in the quadrangle as well.

In the newest of our buildings for graduate students every two suites have a private bath between. Of course, we pride ourselves very much on our plumbing, and I sometimes wonder if we are not becoming almost Roman in our luxuries for bathing: it is possible we have gone too far, and that in time we shall return to more Spartan arrangements; but at present there is no denying the fact that we give nine tenths of our students more than they are accustomed to at home.

Another thing that will strike you is the magnificence of our gymnasiums and the dominating quality of our schools of science. There is really a rivalry amongst our colleges as to which shall have the biggest and most perfectly equipped gymnasium and swimming-pool, but this is partly excused by the fact that our winters are so severe that for three or four months skating, snow-shoeing, and ice-boating are about the only possible forms of out-of-door exercise in the North. Then we have general physical directors, as well as special trainers for the varied forms of athletics, and in many colleges regular and searching examinations of the men for physical and functional weaknesses, and as a result the health of our schools is well above normal. As for our science buildings, you know, as we know only too well, how almost unbalanced we have become in our devotion to practical and "vocational" training, and how obsessed we have become with the mania for natural science. Here at Princeton there is less of this than elsewhere, but two of our newest and most magnificent buildings are devoted, the one to biology, the other to physics, though as yet we have no schools of mechanical and electrical and mining engineering, as happens so often elsewhere.

One novelty you will not notice on the Princeton plan, and that is the clubs and fraternities. We have as many "Greek-Letter Societies" (which are very awful and very secret organizations) as we have colleges, and there are some institutions in America where these fraternity houses almost outnumber the academic buildings themselves. At Princeton no Greek-letter societies are allowed, but there are two old secret organizations, the Whig and the Clio, whose white marble mausoleums form the very centre of the campus, while to the east stretches a great street absolutely lined with the private clubs which grew up when the fraternities were taboo. These clubs take in only a certain number of new members each year; they are distinctly aristocratic in their tone, though aristocratic of a sound and healthy type; and the buildings generally follow the lines of an old and palatial country house.

From all these points of difference you will see, then, that our American university is a very different matter, in its architectural form, from those in this country. Our newest graduate colleges come nearer, as you will see when I show you the now rising buildings for Princeton which lie half a mile to the west.

In the mean time let us examine the beginnings of what has been a notable Gothic renaissance amongst our colleges, and we need not forsake Princeton to do this, for it was here, in the shape of the new library, that it came into being. Alexander Hall had just been completed in the verbose and turgid style that followed the memory of Richardson like a Nemesis, and its architect was given orders to abandon this and revert to what we sometimes call "Oxford Gothic." It was not a style with which he had either sympathy or familiarity, and he produced a work which, while acceptable in its mass and general composition, fails sadly through its coarse scale and its mechanical ornamentation. Almost simultaneously, however, certain new dormitories were put in hand — Blair and Little Halls; and here the architects were two young men of Philadelphia who most unaccountably could think and feel in Gothic terms. I like to record their names whenever I can, — John Stewardson and Walter Cope, — for in addition to being singularly lovable fellows, they were geniuses of no inferior order; they brought into being, at Princeton, Bryn Mawr, and the University of Pennsylvania, structures that are to me singularly beautiful and inspiring, and they left their mark for all time on American architecture. Both are dead, and at a pathetically early age, while the profession of architecture is the poorer thereby.

About the same time a transplanted Englishman, Mr. Vaughan, sometime pupil of that immortal master of the new Gothic, the late

George Bodley, and still with us I am glad to say, began the introduction of the same style into our great preparatory schools, which you here would call "public schools." His work at St. Paul's marked a new era in this category of scholastic architecture, and was continued later in more sumptuous fashion at Groton. My own firm has been following his leadership in the convent school of St. Mary at Peekskill, and the Taft School in Connecticut, while there are innumerable examples of the same sort of thing all over the country.

It was really Cope and Stewardson's work at Princeton that set the pace, however, and so beautiful was it, so convincing as to the possibilities of adapting this perfect style to all modern scholastic requirements, that the Princeton authorities, with a wisdom beyond their generation, passed a law that for the future every building erected there should follow the same general style. "Seventy-nine" Hall, Patton, McCosh, and the Gymnasium followed in quick succession; then came the great Palmer Physical Laboratory, the Biological Laboratory — Guyot Hall — Upper Pyne and Lower Pyne, and a little later, after I had become supervising architect, Campbell Hall, by my own firm, and the altogether wonderful quadrangles of Holder and Hamilton Halls, by Messrs. Day Brothers and Klauder, of Philadelphia. These latter buildings mark one of the very high points we have achieved in Collegiate Gothic in modern times. When the great quads are completed, we shall, I think, confront a masterpiece.

The most recent Princeton work is the great Graduate College my own firm is now building on the crest of a low hill, half a mile from the college campus, and commanding a gently sloping lawn of about eighty acres. This new college is, of course, only for graduate students; it has an endowment of over half a million pounds; it is conceived and organized on the most liberal, cultural, and scholastic lines, far away, indeed, from the popular schemes of "vocational" training; and it should go far toward restoring the balance in favour of sound learning and noble scholarship. The plan shows only the work now in hand, the first quad, with the great hall and its kitchens, together with the

Cleveland Tower, which is a national memorial to one of our greatest Presidents, who spent his years, after retiring from office, in Princeton, as a trustee of the university and a devoted friend of the new Graduate College on the lines that had been determined by its Dean, Dr. West. At present the placing of the great tower seems a little too like that of the Victoria Tower at Westminster to be wholly satisfactory, but in some distant future a second quadrangle will be constructed to the south and east, containing the Chapel, the Library, and quarters for Fellows, which will restore the tower itself to the centre of the composition. Some day, also, a third quad will be developed to the northeast, and then the group will be complete, for the Dean's lodgings, with their private gardens, to the southwest of the great hall, are already under construction.

Let us now turn from Princeton to some others of our many colleges; but before we take up the Gothic tale, let us see what has been done in other stylistic directions, for I would not give you the idea that the restoration of what one of your own great Gothicists, Mr.

Champneys, has called so well the "Oxford Mixture," is all plain sailing, or that splendid work has not been done in other directions. Columbia University in New York — the old King's College of Colonial days — stands, of course, as the noblest type of the pure Classical idea, and its majestical library will always remain a national monument. Unfortunately, the site is crowded and fatally restricted: the mistake was made of fixing this — when the change was necessary a generation ago — too near the outposts of the advancing city, which like a conquering army has already swept up to its gates and miles beyond. For myself I can't imagine a great centre of higher education in the howl and war of a great city, or anywhere, in fact, except in the quiet country or in the village environment it has built for itself, and I fancy another generation will see another moving on of Columbia; and when this happens I venture to predict that, in spite of the grave and scholarly mastery of McKim, Mead, and White's work, the new housing will be on the lines that Oxford and Cambridge have not only made their own, but universal and eternal.

There is little else that is purely Classical amongst our universities, though Carrére and Hastings have built a most engagingly Parisian Alumni Hall at Yale, the Naval Academy at Annapolis is strictly French, and the University of California is growing on scrupulously École des Beaux Arts lines, afar on the Pacific Coast. Georgian, however, has established itself as a determined rival of the "Oxford Mixture," and some of its products are not only logical and lovely, but genuinely scholastic as well. Harvard, as I have said, is beginning to follow this line, and so is Williams, where we ourselves are trying to show we have no hard feelings, by building a Commencement Hall, and a new quadrangle, in this quite characteristically American style. In Virginia, also, we are slowly constructing a great college for women, while we are using the same style for another of our oldest and most famous "preparatory schools" at Exeter, as well as at yet another girls' college, Wheaton, in Massachusetts. Georgian also, with rather quaint Roman elements, has been used by McKim, Mead, and White for the vast War College at Washington, and altogether it is, as we say in our colloquial way, giving Gothic "a run for its money."

The University of Pennysluania shows still more of Cope and Stewardson's wonderful work, though here it is couched in an extremely rich Elizabethan vernacular; and I am sure you will admit that the style is handled in a magnificent and competent fashion. Here it is all red brick and yellow stone, and the same materials are used in Mr. Day's beautifully proportioned and very reserved Gymnasium. Bryn Mawr again is built of the wonderful stone that underlies all Pennsylvania and New Jersey, putting a premium on good architecture. Here in England all building stone is finely dressed, but in America we have adopted the practice of using "ledge stone" for our ashlar, our trimmings only being tooled. Fortunately, we have a wide variety of singularly beautiful stones, ranging in colour through all shades of gray, brown, purple, and tawny, easily obtained, inexpensive and durable. In a way I think we gain a richness in colour and texture that is obtainable in no other way, while we also acquire something of that effect of age, which is, after all, so essential a part of architecture.

Washington University, St. Louis, is later work of this same firm of Cope and Stewardson, after the latter had died, and good as it is, it shows the loss of the peculiar poetry that marked everything Stewardson touched. The plan is exceedingly interesting and very masterly, you will admit. It was laid out *de novo*, and after our college authorities had experienced a change of heart. With Chicago University we come to another of those institutions where the reverse course was followed: here the first buildings were distributed without any regard to architectural effect, and Shepley, Rutan and Coolidge, in taking over the work, have been badly handicapped. This is the most archæological of the "College Gothic" in America, accurate, conservative, and reserved. For contrast consider Mr. Post's "College of the City of New York," which is as poetical, fantastic, and imaginative as the other is austere and cautious. I am afraid I think that here is an example of carrying a good thing too far in the use of one stone for ashlar and another for trimmings. Here the ashlar is almost black (the trap-rock that forms a great dyke along the geological "fault" that forms the Hudson River), while the trimming stones are not stone at all, but a pure white terra-cotta with a surface like ivory. In itself the design is so striking, so forceful, so full of life and spirit, one rather wishes it might have been expressed in materials of greater coherency.

Fortunately, both for education and architecture, practically all our collegiate work is fixed in the country, where there is land enough and we are able to keep down to those modest walls and few ranges of windows that are so essentially a part of the models we now follow: at Princeton, for instance, the residential buildings are seldom more than two stories in height, even when perhaps three would be better; but we are very afraid, and justly, of the aspiring tendencies, in our light-footed land, that lead to the building of Towers of Babel, sometimes, I regret to say, Gothic in style — or rather with passably acceptable Gothic detail. In one instance, however, that of the Union Theological Seminary (a Presbyterian institution), in

New York, strange counsels prevailed as to site and this was chosen well within the city, and where land already possessed an altogether artificial value. As a result the architects, Messrs. Allen and Collens, were confronted with the very grievous necessity of piling up their levels into a total with which, I think, Gothic, either in spirit or in method, has little sympathy. They have a fine chapel, however, and when the enormous corner tower is built, it will probably do much toward reducing the other buildings to a more reasonable frame of mind.

At the beginnings of another theological seminary, Roman Catholic this time, Messrs. Maginnis and Walsh have already completed one building, the tower of which is, I think, very beautiful. The general plan is not yet wholly determined, but it includes a huge parish church and will give a great opportunity for the architects to strike another blow for Roman Catholic Emancipation. I should shrink from trying to give you any faintest idea of the career of architectural crime that has been led by the Roman Church in America until now — and the stars of promise are even yet dim and widely scattered. It has been a carnival of horror unbroken by any ray of light — except, perhaps, St. Patrick's Cathedral and the Paulist Church in New York; but it is much that so good a thing as Boston College should come into existence, and it may serve as a leaven until we Anglicans in America, as you here in England, may have to look alive to prevent Rome outdoing us at our own game, which has always been good architecture and plenty of it.

Near this Roman college, another great institution is rising, not strictly collegiate, though certainly educational, the "Perkins Institution for the Blind," where Mr. R. C. Sturgis is developing a singularly personal and intimate piece of semi-domestic Gothic. In fact, as I said at the beginning, good Gothic is encroaching steadily on the preserves of Classicist, Boulevardier, and Colonial, and this in spite of the fact that, with the single exception of Harvard, every one of our schools of architecture absolutely disregards every type and phase of Gothic, both in design and in theory. Of course, it can't quite be suppressed in history and archæology, but it is treated rather as the madcap escapade of a callow youth, and passed over as lightly as possible. In spite of this, architects do appear who love Gothic, and, what is more, know about it also. Religion clamours for it, education annexes it, and even, in one instance, the Government of the United States itself accepted it with alacrity, and has found it not half so bad as it looked. For an end, therefore, of this casual showing, I want to place before you some views of the United States Military Academy at West Point, of which, as a military training-school, we are so inordinately and so justly proud. I cannot begin to give you any idea of the extravagant beauty of the site of West Point: it is like the loveliest part of the Rhine, only bolder and more dramatic. Mountains rise from the river on either hand, deeply forested, Storm-King and Dunderberg lifting highest of all; and on a narrow plateau, one hundred and fifty feet above the river, stands the Academy, its buildings forming a rampart along the cliff and creeping up the mountain-sides all around. Of course there was n't anything one could do there *except* Gothic, — of sorts, — though others had thought differently, as one who built there a lovely pagan fane like a dream of Imperial Rome. Moreover, most of the old work was pseudo-Gothic, and it had made a tradition, — everything does this at West Point, I am glad to say, — so it was not startling after all that our Classical Government should have endorsed a Gothic school.

I am not sure they got it: I think the chapel on its crag, dominating the whole group, would pass, though it surely is not archæological; the site is compelling, however, and really what we tried to do was to translate the rocks and trees and ribbed cliffs into architectural form. In the interior there is perhaps something more of the scholastic quality: in any case it is all honest masonry throughout, — floor, walls, and vault, — and it ought to stand for all time. Just what the cavalry and artillery buildings may be, I don't know, nor does it much matter: they are an attempt to express outwardly their function and in the simplest terms; the stables sweep in an enormous arc around one side of the cavalry plain, and at the back, against the towering hills, are the barracks, one for each branch of the service. The riding hall is no more, architecturally, than a rampart of rock, heavily buttressed, and six hundred feet in length, a dimension that is prolonged to the south by the tower, and the power-house that breaks down step by step, along the coal-conveyor, to the water level and the railway tunnel. The cadet barracks are the result of an *amour* (perhaps illicit) between ironclad military regulations and a very free and easy Gothic, but their interminable ranges of windows and buttresses show not unpicturesquely through the great trees that border the Infantry Plain. The gymnasium is something freer still, but not unpleasing in its colour, of tawny brick of a kind of velvet texture, and creamy stone trimmings. Unfortunately some of the most important work is not yet begun. There are scores of semi-detached quarters for married officers, from many of which the views are such as one crosses continents to see; but the new academic building is not yet finished, while no funds have been made available for the vast quadrangles of the quartermaster's department, the cadet headquarters which will, from the plain, form the structural base for the chapel (though this will be well behind and above), the hotel, and—most needed of all—the staff headquarters. This latter group will terminate the main axis, which will stretch a full half-mile from the landing on the upper level at the elevator tower and below the hotel, past the infirmary, between the old and the new academic buildings connected by their vast triumphal arch with its niched statues, past the enormous post headquarters, and so across the middle of the Infantry Plain. The group will be made up of residential quarters for the superintendent, commandant of cadets, quartermaster, adjutant, and surgeon, all grouped around an open court that contains the state apartments of the President, the secretary of war, and distinguished guests. There will be a great tower pierced by an arched sally-port, a banqueting-room vaulted and walled in stone, state reception-rooms, and all the other accommodations necessary at a place that appeals with singular force to all the people of the Republic, from its Chief Magistrate down to the humblest taxpayer.

Lacking these buildings, West Point is, of

course, quite incomplete, but it is worth seeing even now, and for my own part I think, of the finished buildings, the post headquarters is not the least interesting. It is built on the edge of the cliff, and the entrance by the base gate is four stories below the main court, which is entered from the upper level. It is a pretty big building, but it is wholly occupied by the administration of the Academy and the military museum, and I want particularly to say that, massive as it is, it is all real masonry: it is no steel-frame skeleton clothed indifferently with a veneering of masonry; it is all of stone dug from the reservation cliffs and shot down to these lower levels.

And the same is true not only of the rest of the buildings at West Point, but of practically all the other work I have shown you as well. We do, indeed, indulge in skeleton construction and reinforced concrete and other structural expedients and substitutes, but deep in our racial consciousness, as in that of all other Anglo-Saxon peoples, is the solid conviction that, after all, there are but three real things in the world, — the home, the school, and the

Church, — and that when we are dealing with eternal verities honest and enduring construction is alone admissible. And it is to the same consciousness, I think, that we may attribute the very universal return to Gothic of some form for our churches and our colleges and our schools. After all, there have never been but three real styles of architecture in the West, noble in impulse, organic in structure, perfect in detail; and these three are Greek, Byzantine, and Gothic: everything else is either a patois or a form of slang. Greek and Byzantine are in essence alien to our blood and temper, and Gothic alone remains. Over-seas, flushed with a new and half-unconscious recognition of the revolution that is slowly lifting the world out of materialism to the high free levels of a new idealism and spirituality, we instinctively revert to the very style which came into being to voice the old idealism and the old spirituality of the great Christian Middle Ages. Thus far we have, perhaps, done little more than reproduce; recording our reverence for the great works of our common ancestors, in buildings that hold closely to type. We have not hammered out our own intimate style, or national and contemporary architecture, any more than have any other modern races and peoples; but this will come by and by. At present we architects are, I conceive, no longer as in the past the mouthpiece of a people, creating the visible form for a great dominating social impulse that is the mark of supreme civilization: rather are we the voices crying in the wilderness, the pioneers of the vanguard of the new life, the men who re-create from antiquity the beauty that is primarily educational, that so it may work subtly through the consciousness of those who come under its influence, slowly building up a new civilization that, when it has come full tide, will burst the shell of archæological forms and come forth in its new and significant and splendid shape.

We have not now, nor have had for three centuries, a civilization that demanded or could create such artistic expression; but the light is already on the edges of the high hills, and we know that a new dawn is at hand. In the mean time, like the monks in the dim monasteries of the Dark Ages, we cherish and conserve all that was great in our greatest past, building as well as we may new Oxfords and new Westminster Abbeys, new Lincolns, new Richmond Castles, new Haddon Halls, not for a last new word in architectural expression, but as schoolmasters and as prophets, content with the educational work we are accomplishing, leaving to our successors the equal but not more honourable task of voicing in novel and adequate form the new civilization we are helping to create.

VII

THE MINISTRY OF ART

VII

THE MINISTRY OF ART[1]

ARCHITECTURE, even in a title, can hardly be disassociated from the other component parts of that wonderful gift of God that, in our indifferent use of words, we denominate "art." In each one of them, whether it be sculpture, painting, or architecture, poetry, music, the drama, or ceremonial, there is, of course, one peculiar mode whereby it manifests itself, the instrument of its operation; but each of these is but a dialect of a normal language; together they are the Pentecostal tongues through which the Holy Spirit manifests Himself in a peculiar way to all nations and kindreds and peoples. Art is not only a function of the soul, an inalienable heritage of man, an attribute of all godly and righteous society; it is also the language of all spiritual ventures and experiences, while, more potently than any other of the works of man, it proclaims the

[1] Read before the American Church Congress, Troy, N.Y.

glory of God, revealing in symbolical form some measure of that absolute truth and that absolute beauty that are His being.

Through all the varied qualities of this sevenfold mystery of art runs one unchanging and unchangeable principle, and the nature of this principle we must define before we consider the particularities of one art alone and the scope and potency of its service.

In this necessity there is, let us admit, something unnatural. Never in the past has there been a great art that was clearly conscious of its nature: none that by taking thought has added one cubit to its stature. Art that is self-conscious halts on the perilous rim of artifice. The intensive activities of art analysis and art education have brought into being never an art and never an artist of the measure of the artist and the art of a past so absorbed in spiritual adventures and material accomplishments that it lacked the time for self-analysis. And yet, so novel is the basis of our contemporary life, so severed from the spiritual succession of history, so bound by the chains of analysis to the rock of definition, we are compelled by circumstance to analyze and define as never before; nor can we keep our curious hands from the Pandora's box of very mystery itself, forgetting that the lifted lid means, not the clear revealing of strange and hidden wonders, but their instant and implacable flight.

The curious inquiries of Calvin wrought hopeless havoc with the heavenly vision of St. Augustine; the insolent brutalities of eugenics are the Nemesis of wholesome humanity; the picking and stealing fingers of the Renaissance broke the Psyche wings of art; and yet, in defiance of precedent, we essay again the excuseless and the impossible. What do we mean by "art," the thing once so instinctive that it needed no more definition than did "thought" or "action" or "prayer"? Well, we have made of an instinct an accessory, and since such it has become, and since it has almost been lost in the process, we may, in defiance of fate, define again.

Now, none of us, here and now, means what the word has been held to imply since the dawn of the debatable epoch above named. We know it is neither a commodity, a form of amusement, an amenity of life, or even the guinea stamp of civilization. Of course, it is, in a measure, the last, to the extent that it is not a product, but a result of that quality of life that is the manifestation, in time and space, of righteous impulses and modes of human activity. In its high estate it is never a by-product of barbarism; though it sometimes seems so, as in the case of the Renaissance where we find most noble art synchronizing with an almost complete collapse of Christian civilization. The same thing has happened before, and will again, for while all sound and wholesome and well-balanced life of necessity expresses itself in that instinctive art which is the art of the people, this great art product seldom achieves its perfect fruition until after the great impulse that created it has broken down and yielded to inevitable degeneration. Thus we find the most splendid, if not the most noble, Gothic architecture blossoming in the fourteenth century after the high tide of mediævalism had begun to ebb; while painting reached its climax during the unspeakable barbarism of the epoch of the Medici and the Borgia; Shakespeare and his circle — soul-children of the Catholic Middle Ages — weaving the glamour of their divine genius over the decadent era of Elizabeth; and music, most subtle of all the arts, giving to Protestant Germany a glory that by her intrinsic nature she could scarcely claim.

In these and the similar cases in earlier history there is no discrepancy, no ground for arguing that art is a natural product either of heresy, immorality, or disorder: born of righteousness of impulse and sanity of life, it is the longest to endure, lingering like the afterglow long past the actual setting of the sun, — a memory and at the same time a hope.

In a time that is curiously prone to false estimates of comparative values, that is positively triumphant in its capacity for misjudging the quality of essentials, we measure nearly all the arts by the dazzling products of the last great geniuses who linger beyond their time, quite forgetting the centuries of less splendid activity that, manifesting, as they did, the art instinct of a people, were intrinsically nobler, and in themselves were the energy behind the coruscating stars of a rocket that had already burst.

In judging art, in determining its function, in estimating its potency, it is necessary, therefore, to go behind the evidences of Rouen and the chapel of Henry VII, of Botticelli and Tintoretto, of Shakespeare and Marlowe, of Bach and Beethoven, — to name only the latest of the great periods of history, — and to regard that wonder-work of the great centuries from Gregory VII to the exile at Avignon, which is the true product of a triumphant Christian civilization.

And so regarded, we find that art, as I have already said, is neither a commodity, nor a form of amusement, nor an amenity of life, but a wonderful attribute of man who is made in God's image, a subtle language, and a mystery that, in its nature, we may with reverence call sacramental.

This, I believe, is the secret and the function of art. It is a language of divine revelation, the great sequence of mystical symbols that alone are adequate and efficient when the soul of man enters into the infinite realm of eternal truth. To each its proper tongue: to reason, dealing with phenomena and their knowable relations, the language of natural science and of natural philosophy; to the soul, by the grace of God penetrating beyond the veil that limits our mortal sense, achieving the quest of the Holy Grail of ultimate truth, the language of art, which is beauty, sacramentally comprehended, sacramentally employed. Other language there is none: before the Beatific Vision, even though now we see it as in a glass, darkly, even though the symbol alone is all our undeveloped spirituality can apprehend, the language that is so adequate for dealing with the mere accidents and phenomena of the Absolute fails utterly before the dim vision of the substance that lies behind, informing all. Natural science and natural philosophy are sufficient unto themselves: they need no aid from the Pentecostal tongues of art; but religion, which deals alone with ultimate realities, finds in the "form of sound words" only her panoply of defence against the insolence of insubordinate reason; for her self-revelation, for the communicating of her infinitely higher and more subliminal reason, she turns to the tongue God gave her to this end, to painting, sculpture, and architecture; to poetry, music, the drama, and ceremonial; to art, the great symbol; to art, the language of the soul.

Postulating this of art in its intrinsic nature, let me say at once that I do not confine the thing itself simply to the great arts already named; as there are seven sacraments defined by the Church, while nevertheless the sacramental quality extends, in varying degrees, into infinite ramifications throughout creation, so art itself, which is made up of seven major modes, reaches out into innumerable fields of potent activity. Beauty is the instrument of art; without it art does not exist, and wherever beauty is used either for self-revelation or for the communicating of spiritual energy, there is art, whether it be in the majestic modes of music and architecture, or in the modest ministry of woodcarving or embroidery. The existence and manifestation of beauty is the one test, the philosopher's stone that transmutes the base metal of reason into the fine gold of spiritual revelation.

Now, I do not mean to involve myself in the perilous definition of this mystical and incomprehensible thing, beauty; says St. Thomas à Kempis, in writing of the sublime Mystery of the Catholic Faith, "'T were well not to inquire too curiously into the nature of this holy sacrament"; and the same warning may well be held in mind when we approach the mystery of beauty. It *is*, and its operations are acknowledged; this is really all we need to know. In this paper I am supposed to deal only with this operation, and in the one category of architecture, so all that is needed is the confession we all can make that beauty exists and that it is the great symbolic language of the soul, whether it manifests itself through colour or form or light and shade, through tone, melody, harmony and rhythm, or through any combination of these, or any other of the numberless modes of its expression.

It may be said that not the half of art is thus specifically spiritual in its activity; that in whole schools and for long periods of time art of noble quality is followed and determined solely for the sheer joy of pleasurable sensations. This we may admit, for *conscious* revelation of higher things is no essential part of art; my only contention is that it alone has been so used, and may be again, even though for generations we may, in our hardness of heart, deny the very existence of any realm of truth beyond that accidental domain of the material and the conditioned, which from time to time obsesses men with the delusion of its own finality. And even here I think the thesis might be defended that this very sensuous satisfaction, as we call it, is not sensuous at all, but the blind answering of an atrophied soul to a spiritual stimulus, the noble nature of which is disregarded or denied. The obvious melodies of popular music, the rudimentary colour-harmonies of popular painting, the superficial jingles of popular verse, are pleasurable to those who like them, not because of some satisfying titillation of the sensory nerves, but because they, even they, are informed with some faint and far-blown scent of mystical fields, and strange gardens seen in forgotten dreams; because each one, however narrow the vista it reveals, is in some sense one of those

> "Magic casements opening on the foam
> Of perilous seas, by faëry lands forlorn" —

that are the avenues of spiritual revelation through the mystical agency of art.

On this very matter writes that beautiful soul, Sir Thomas Browne: "For even that vulgar and Tavern-Musick, which makes one man merry, another mad, strikes in me a deep fit of devotion, and a profound contemplation of the First Composer. There is something in it of Divinity more than the ear discovers: it is an Hieroglyphical and shadowed lesson of the whole World, and creatures of God; such a melody to the ear, as the whole World, well understood, would afford the understanding. In brief, it is a sensible fit of that harmony which intellectually sounds in the ears of God."

This by the way, for our inquiry is not here, and I try to return to the path that may, in the end, lead at the very last to our subject.

I have said enough to indicate what I mean when I speak of all art as the natural, and, indeed, the only adequate, expression in time and space of spiritual things. If it is this, then it follows of necessity that it is the ordained language of religion, for religion, through theology, is the divine science which is higher than all natural sciences, in that it deals with Absolute Truth through perfectly adequate agencies, while the natural sciences deal only with finite phenomena through agencies adequate to this end and to this alone. It follows, then, that preëminently and in a very special fashion art is, or should be, a matter of absolutely vital importance to religion, since it is ordered by God Himself as its mode of visible manifestation. As a matter of fact, this always has been so from the very beginnings of recorded history. "God has never left Himself without a witness"; and even in the ethnic religions of antiquity, or the paganism that preceded the Incarnation, or in the pseudo-religious philosophies of the East, the dim witnesses of God have made for themselves out of art in all its forms witnesses before men of whatever shadowy glimmerings of truth were given to them. Babylon, Assyria, Egypt, all wrought for themselves great art, but always the beginnings were at the hands of priests and prophets, and however great the secular art that ensued, always its greatest glories were achieved in religious service. And so through history, century after century, through the fastidious and exquisite temples of Greece and the half-barbarian "grandeur that was Rome," to the solemn basilicas of Constantine, the golden and glimmering shrines of Justinian, the grave majesty of the churches of Charlemagne, the towering abbeys of Frank and Norman Benedictines, the first fine Gothic of the Cistercian monasteries, to the crowning glory of the mediæval cathedrals of France and the abbeys of England. Even when civilization was breaking down under the assaults of the new paganism after the exile at Avignon and the fall of Constantinople, it was religion, whatever we may think of its momentary condition, that was still, through the visible Church, leading the van in the building-up of a new though fictitious form of art; and it was not until the Reformation that, for the first time in the history of the world, organized religion turned against art, and, denying its virtue or its efficacy, devoted itself to the destruction of what it had created and what had been, in solemn fact, one of its most potent agencies of operation. And then followed, also for the first time in history, that ominous thing, the extinction of all art, of every kind whatever, as an attribute of human life, as a heritage of civilization. Indeed, what actually ensued was worse even than extinction: it was the substitution, first, of something with little beauty and with no art at all in place of the perfect beauty man already had perfectly made manifest; then the wild yet deliberate beating down and utter destruction of these dumb memorials of a great material and spiritual past; and finally, the setting-up, for the worship of degenerate society, of the brazen images of ugliness. A stranger and more ominous thing than this history has hardly recorded. We have seen, and many times, the perishing of great civilizations: the flowering of art during some epoch of splendid development, and its slow dissolution after that epoch had yielded to the law of the world, which is the law of degeneration, in opposition to the law of the spirit, which is the law of regeneration and development. We have seen the exquisite art of Greece go down in the wake of Greek civilization, while the art of Rome that followed on was immeasurably less noble and complete. In its turn we have beheld the fall of Rome and the coming of the Dark Ages, with even here, at the height of such culture as came during a barbarian cycle, art that was art still, though less admirable even than that which developed under "the drums and tramplings of three conquests." Then at last this also was gone with the dying of the "false dawn" of Carlovingian civilization, and night fell again, deeper than ever before; night that was to be dispelled for centuries, a little later, when the mingling of Northern blood with the great life-current of a regenerated monasticism was to make possible the first great triumph of Christian civilization.

Time upon time it has seemed that art has been lost; but even in the deepest depths it has struggled for light, and never once has it been false to its own nature. There might be little, and that little poor, but its impulse was always right, until that great world-drama (the three acts of which we call the Renaissance, the Reformation, and the Revolution) took possession of the stage; and since then the tale has been different. The Renaissance, by its false doctrine of the sufficiency of the intellect, set up a scholastic and artificial theory of the nature of beauty and the function of art; the Reformation, by its substitution of a manufactured religion for that of God's Revelation, dried up the springs of spiritual energy which are the source of the art-impulse; the Revolution shook the very foundations of religious society and established economic conditions in which art could no longer endure; while all these cataclysms, as a by-product of their activity, annihilated a good half of the monuments of past generations, and denied the virtue of the poor remainder they did not destroy.

It was the greatest break-down on record, and the results were commensurate with the cause. Art was gone, for the first time in history; and with the opening of the nineteenth century not only was the world more empty than ever before, but there were false gods in every shrine, hideous idols of the worship of ugliness and lies. Here and there was a voice crying in the wilderness, but when it became audible over the din of an uncouth saturnalia, it was the voice of a painter, a poet, or a musician; sculptor and architect had "none so mean as to do them reverence."

And now the wheel has come full turn, and everywhere is a feverish effort at artistic restoration. We are ashamed, and we seek for the wherewithal to cover our æsthetic nakedness; more than this, the old virus is working itself out: the fruits of the Renaissance, Reformation, and Revolution have been eaten, the good is by way of being assimilated, the evil rejected, and the gray dawn of a new day lightens on the hills. In spite of the curial ineptitudes of Rome, the invincible Erastianism of the East, the uncertainties of our own estate; in spite of the momentary triumph of atheism and anarchy in France, the outbreak of unearthly heresies and superstitions in Russia and New England, and the apparent victory of secularism in education; in spite of the ethical, political, industrial, and economic disorder, the doom of the post-Renaissance era is sealed, and in the midst of all our uncertainties one thing is gloriously certain, and that is that a new epoch is dawning when religion will once more achieve its due supremacy over man and nations, the Catholic Faith regain its beneficent dominion over the souls that God made in His own image.

It is this conviction, whether avowed or hidden, whether conscious or latent, that lies at the base of the great turning of religion to art once more in these latest days. Not the desire of emulation, not the hunger for refinements of culture, but the dawning consciousness that each one of the arts is by right a paladin of the new crusade, that they are all, by the nature given them by God, soldiers of the Cross, and that their hearts and their swords are not lightly to be despised in the new winning of the world to Christ.

Michelet has somewhere said that "history is only a series of resurrections"; and this is what the Church is doing to-day — returning to the old and tried methods of the past, when the builder and painter and carver, the musician and poet and maker of liturgies, marched side by side with the prophet and monk and missionary into the strongholds of barbarism and infidelity, putting into visible and audible form the faith they practised.

No other course was possible. Since beauty is the revelation of all that lies beyond the horizon of our finite vision, art, which is beauty organized and made operative, becomes the great language of the soul, and therefore it is crushed, mutilated, impotent when it remains in bondage to material things, while without it religion is shorn of one of her greatest agencies of self-expression and of influence. This is the meaning of the wonderful revival of religious art of every kind that began simultaneously with the spiritual upheaval of the Oxford Movement, and has kept pace, step by step, with the growing consciousness of her Catholic heritage which, for now three quarters of a century, has penetrated the Church of the English-speaking race. This is the meaning of the new life in religious painting and sculpture; in glass-making and metal-working and embroidery; in architecture, music, and ceremonial. We look, sometimes with amusement, sometimes with horror, on the ecclesiastical fabrics of the early nineteenth century, on the barren and hideous forms, the apologetic music, the thin and enervated ceremonial. Now we, and not we alone, but all Protestantism with us, are building churches as near in spirit and in form to those of the great Middle Ages as the somewhat limited capacities of our architects will permit: we demand the glass of Chartres and York, the sculptures of Amiens and Wells, the gold and silver and brass and iron of Hildesheim and Venice and Dalmatia, the pictures of Umbria, the music of Milan, the vestments of the treasuries of Spain. Daily our ceremonial grows richer and more beautiful, and its widening ring takes in, one after another, men and places that but a few years ago were staunch defenders, if not of Calvinistic theology, at least of Calvinistic art. Even the old shibboleth of "Romanizing, Romanizing," is heard no more, for its absurdity is recognized, and the basic impulse of religious art is seen to be other than a preliminary symptom of disaffection. It is not because we want something that Rome alone has got, but because at last we know we have it also, the thing itself, that we return to our sister, Beauty, and call upon her once again to cry to all the manifold products of God's hand, "O all ye works of the Lord, bless ye the Lord, praise Him and magnify Him forever."

The theological peculiarities of Geneva and Edinburgh can adequately be communicated by the spoken and unadorned word: the marvellous mysteries of the Catholic Faith breathe themselves into the spiritual consciousness through the mediumship of art.

To every movement, then, toward the restoration of diplomatic relations between religion and art, the Church must give her earnest support. Everywhere the artist and the craftsman are looking wistfully toward the old-time mistress of their art. Usually they have lost their faith, and they are not wholly to blame for it; but in their art lies the possibility of their conversion, or at least the assurance that, accepted, it will be easier for those that follow to regain their faith, or hold it whole and intact. To all the workers in all the arts the Church must now go, saying, "We made you; we forsook you; we are sorry; and now we need you again: give us of your best that we may offer it on the altar of God."

"The best." Here, perhaps, lies the kernel of it all. For centuries we have taken the worst, and as little of that as possible; now we take anything that comes along, not from perversity but from lack of knowledge, and from a certain innocent trustfulness that takes a man — and particularly an artist — at his own valuation, or at least at the valuation placed upon him by some person or thing of which we stand in awe. Late Italian Mass music and decadent ceremonial; plausible and loudly heralded stained glass of barbaric splendour; commercial products in metal and woodwork, saccharine statues — sometimes of plaster — of the type dear to the heart of the Latin "parrocchio"; imitation Gothic architecture — also sometimes of plaster, with a little harmless, necessary steel or iron encased within. We want the real thing, the real beauty, the real art, but the trouble is we sometimes can be induced to accept a substitute, while sometimes also the best of us know too well what we like, and this is always dangerous.

The first battle has been won — the battle for Beauty; we know now that this we must have; now let us establish the victory by winning the battle for Truth.

And this does not mean the easy victory over plaster and papier-mâché, gold-leaf and lacquer, imitation marble, steel covered with concrete, and all the other substitutes that are now so tempting to the eye hungry for beauty combined with the emaciated purse. It means the far more arduous battle for the fundamental truth of æsthetic ideals, for art that shall be significant, and vital with the breath of the great art of the past.

It is not the fault of the priest, or the building committee, or the altar society that here we so often fail; it is the fault, in great measure, of the artist; but I honestly believe he himself is only a victim of that most pernicious and devil-engendered principle of the present age, namely, "Give the people what they want." Of course, any society that acts on that basis has its ending in the pit of perdition; but this we do not see with perfect clarity, and so the artist prostitutes his God-given art to the false ideal of what is demanded of him. He is wrong; no one nowadays wants anything but the best in art — which is one of the most encouraging signs in a dubious day; but this demand is not always couched in unmistakable terms. Be specific, make it clear that you look on the artist as a minister in minor orders, and that on him alone rests the obligation to make his work, in however small a degree, a revelation of spiritual truth, and I do not think he will fail you.

I do not mean that as yet any artist can safely be given his head; least of all, the architect. Art is still in bondage to that spirit of the Renaissance-Reformation-Revolution the Church has now freed herself from to so surprising a degree; but I *do* mean that the time has come when a principle only may safely be enunciated, the details being left wholly to the artist. It is not so long ago that priests who had read Parker's "Glossary," or some handbook on church-building, or had spent a summer in England, felt it their duty to instruct an architect as to the working-out of his plans, even in some cases demanding that some church or other in England should be duplicated. Well, this was bad enough, but I dare say better than the terrible things that might have happened — and did happen, for that matter — when the architect was permitted to give free rein to his fervid imagination. In any case, this time has gone, and in spite of the schools of architecture there are now many artists of every kind — and particularly architects — who may safely be trusted to do honourable and competent work. Nevertheless, there is still one function that the priest, or, better still, the Church, must perform, and that is the laying-down of the fundamental law of all religious art.

What is this law? It is a very simple one, namely, that religious art must express, not the predilections of one man, or the arbitrary theories of a school, but the Church herself; in other words, a divine institution unchangeable in essentials, infinitely adaptable in everything else. And this means that whatever is done must be faithful, first of all, to the universal laws of Christian art; then, that it must preserve an unbroken continuity with the art of our own blood and race; and finally, that it must declare itself of our own time as to the accidents of its expression.

Several principles develop from this: under the first heading we are forced back five centuries to the time when Christian art came to an end; across the desert wastes of Protestantism and the opulent gardens of neo-paganism, back to the Middle Ages, when the living stream, that had refreshed a thirsty land from before the days of Hellas and Byzantium, disappeared below the surface into some subterranean channel wherefrom comes now only the murmur of troubled waters impatient for release. So far as the art expression of religion is concerned, nothing has happened since the fall of Constantinople in which we need display any particular interest. Back to mediævalism we must go, and begin again. And as to continuity, that indispensable succession that alone insures the vitality of art while it parallels that apostolical succession which alone insures the divine vitality of the Catholic Church, it means that we are not at liberty to pick and choose among the tentative styles of a crescent Christianity, but that we must return to the one style our forefathers at last created for the full expression of their blood and faith. Lombard we may like, or Byzantine, or Norman, or Romanesque, but they are not for us, for they were stepping-stones only, not accomplished facts. Those that were of the South or the East are of alien blood. Our Church and we ourselves are of the North, northern. We are of them that purged the world of a great paganism, dead, and infecting all Europe with the miasma of its corruption. Frank and Teuton, Norman and Burgundian, Celt and Saxon and Dane are in our blood and bone and our very flesh, and for the major part of what we are we owe an everlasting debt to this fierce blood of the Baltic shores, tamed and turned into righteous courses by the monks of St. Benedict, St. Robert, St. Bernard, and St. Norbert.

We forget it all, for a time, but we return at last, and as now perhaps the most significant thing in the development of our own moiety of the Church is the restoration of that monasticism which was the engendering fire of Christian mediævalism, so by inevitable analogy we return to the art that blossomed in the gardens the monks made in the wilderness; to the heritage of our name and race, the Gothic of France and England and of all our own north countries, washed by our own north seas. Yet there is danger in this — the danger of archæological dry rot. We must begin somewhere; we no longer have within ourselves the power of artistic generation; and even if we had, if we could produce an art like that of Paris or Canterbury or York out of our own inner selves, we should lack the right, for we must above all things show that our religion stretches, without a break, through mediævalism and the Dark Ages, to Calvary. Gothic architecture and Gothic art do this, for in them are gathered up and perfected all the tentative efforts of all Christendom; but if we stop there we deny the Faith, for we know that in accordance with the promise of Christ He is with His Church even unto the end of the world, and that through the abiding presence of the Holy Spirit she is being led into all truth. The Christian life is a life of progressive development; the life of the Church is no other; and little by little new aspects of old wonders are opened before our eyes. Therefore, our art must content itself with no finalities; it must grow ever and onward, from the highest point thus far it has reached, the mountain summit of mediævalism, from whose cloud-encircled top dim visions already unroll of still loftier summits, accessible at last, once we forsake the mistaken path that long ago opened out, broad and inviting, only to disappear in the morass of artificial paganism. And so our new art, refounded on the old, must be mobile, adaptable, sensitive to all righteous influences, repellent of all that are evil; not a simulacrum, but a living thing.

Is this too much to ask? Greater has been before, and with faith we may move mountains.

The part that art is to play in the rebuilding of a new civilization is hardly to be estimated in words, and of all the arts the one that is destined to do the greatest work is architecture. Why this is so I confess I do not know, but so it has been in the past. There is some strange quality in architecture that makes its spiritual efficiency dominant over the other arts. Music is more poignant, painting more human in its appeal, while each art in its turn exerts some special influence beyond the province of the others. Architecture binds them in one, harmonizing, controlling, directing them, and lifting them up in a great structural *Te Deum*.

A perfect church, within whose walls is passing the ordered pageantry unnumbered generations have built up in beauty, and through the seven arts, to do honour and reverence to the

Creator and Redeemer of the world, there present in the Holy Sacrament of the altar, is the greatest work of man. Into it enters every art raised now to the highest point of achievement, and as architecture, painting, and sculpture assemble for the building of the tabernacle itself, so do music, poetry, the drama, and ceremonial gather into another great work of art, that prefigures the infinite wonder of Heaven itself.

And we threw it all away, once, in our blindness of heart and contempt of God's word and commandment: blowing up the matchless fabrics with gunpowder; beating out the jewelled windows and shattering with hammer and axe the fretted altars and shrines and tombs and chiselled images of saints and martyrs, even the Crucifix itself, the sign of our Redemption; filching the jewels from vestments and sacred vessels, casting consecrated gold and silver into the melting-pot, turning copes and chasubles into bed-hangings, and altar-cloths into chair-cushions, leaving the few churches we did not destroy barren, empty, desolated.

Now we are doing what we can by way of

amendment. We are handicapped by the deeds of our fathers, and by their consequences, but the restoration must be accomplished, however arduous the effort.

And the reward is worthy the effort. Create in imagination the figure of what may be again: cathedrals like those of Paris and Chartres and Gloucester and Exeter; sculptures like the marshalled saints of Amiens and Wells, pictures and altar-pieces like those of Giotto and Fra Angelico; windows that rival those of Bourges and York; the beating of sublime Gregorian chants like the echo of heavenly harmonies; and ceremonial that absorbs half of the regenerated arts, composing them into a whole that is the perfection of all that man can do to honour in material and sensible form the central mystery of the Catholic Faith.

Once more at the hand of man all the works of the Lord shall praise Him and magnify Him forever, and from every cathedral or monastery or parish church shall go out the vast, subtle, insistent missionary influence of art, again restored to her due place as the handmaid of religion; breaking down that pride of intellect that will not yield to intellectual attack; winning souls hungry but defiant; dissolving the barriers that man in his insolence has reared to make of no avail the prayer of Christ that all His children might be made one; manifesting to the world the Absolute Truth and Beauty that are the Revelation of God. Architecture, with all the arts, is the God-given language of religion. It has been too long in bondage to the world; let it now serve God again through the Holy Catholic Church.

THE END